$19.95

CN01573343

Julia Sheppard started her career as a football reporter on *Rugby Leaguer* magazine and then joined the Sydney *Daily Mirror* as a sports journalist. Later she worked for the Sydney *Daily Telegraph* and *The Sun* as a general news reporter covering two royal commissions: the Ananda Marga Inquiry and the Chamberlain Royal Commission. She was involved in covering the Anita Cobby investigation and later all court cases relating to the murder. In March, 1988, she joined 'Hinch at 7' as a senior researcher and now works in news and current affairs at Channel 10.

Julia resides in Sydney with her husband Phillip Sigsworth.

For every family who believes that tragic events, such as those recounted in this book, are so far removed from their lives that they can never happen to them.

The best parts of our lives can be found in the hearts of those who loved us.

SOMEONE ELSE'S DAUGHTER

THE LIFE AND DEATH OF ANITA COBBY

By

Julia Sheppard

IRONBARK PRESS

First published 1991 by Ironbark Press
This edition published in Ironbark by Pan Macmillan
Australia Pty Limited
St Martins Tower, 31 Market Street, Sydney

Reprinted 1991 (twice), 1993, 1994 (twice)

National Library of Australia
cataloguing-in-publication data:

Julia Sheppard
Someone Else's Daughter – The Life and Death of Anita Cobby

ISBN 1 875471 02 2

1. Cobby, Anita. 2. Murder – NSW – Sydney. 3. Nurses – NSW – Sydney – Biography. I. Title.

364.1523099441

Design Concept: Robbylee Phelan
Finished Art: Kylie Prats
Edited by Larry Writer
Typeset by Photoset Computer Services
Printed in Australia by McPherson's Printing Group

Foreword

When I was first assigned to cover the investigation into the murder of Anita Cobby, in February, 1986, I was working as a journalist for the Sydney *Sun* newspaper. Anita's body had been found a week before. With a dozen other reporters that day, I waited on the footpath outside Blacktown police station for a development in the hunt for her killer or killers. I was there to assist our regular police roundsman, Simon Bouda, who was exhausted from covering the story around the clock since it had broken.

At that stage, this murder, although judged important by the large number of police assigned to solve it, didn't strike any of us reporters as being so very different from other crimes against innocent people. But when the first three men were arrested, it hit home to me the complex ways in which the murder of this young nurse had affected our community. Standing there outside the police station, in the middle of the mayhem, with everyday Australians: grandmothers, children, men in suits and mothers with babies, all screaming for revenge, was like nothing I had experienced. These were ordinary people like you and me. People who had never known Anita personally but prepared to make their outrage known. Why did this crime move our nation like no other?

The next week, after all five had been arrested, I was sent to the Blacktown home of Anita's parents, Grace and Garry Lynch. I remember walking up the front steps and feeling like I was intruding on their privacy, another media vulture. They had had journalists interviewing them just about every day since their daughter's body had been found. I knocked and was given a wonderfully warm reception from Grace and Garry. They spoke of how other journalists and cameramen had been kind to them, how the police were caring, how good the family support had been.

They were the nicest people, ordinary people, who had been forced to wear this incredible sorrow for the world to see. Mrs Lynch was sweet and shy. She reminded me very much of my own mother. Mr Lynch was unashamedly emotional at times when speaking about Anita. I thought, yes, my own father would cry too, if it had been me who had been savagely killed. Their daughter was 26 when she died. I was 26 too. We were both born in the same year and the same month. But I would grow old.

For most journalists, years spent covering crimes and accident scenes dull the senses to the sufferings of victims. But after hours and hours of note-taking at this trial, tears sprang to my eyes when the Government Medical Officer Dr Joe Malouf expressed the belief that Anita Cobby had been conscious at the time her throat was slashed. It would have taken two minutes for her to bleed to death. I looked at my radio colleague, Felcity Moffatt, sitting beside me. On hearing the same evidence she took a sharp breath and whispered, "Oh, no!" I tried to imagine what terror and helplessness this girl must have felt lying there on the ground in that paddock on that hot summer night with her savage injuries and knowing there was not a damn thing she could do to save herself. Did she think of her family, her friends, her estranged husband, or perhaps, mercifully, her poor mind was numbed from the shock of what she had endured.

The trial of the killers of Anita Cobby was one of the largest I have covered and certainly it attracted massive media attention. In the months before I had been in the Northern Territory for the Morling Royal Commission of Inquiry into the convictions of Lindy and Michael Chamberlain. But even the massive attention of that inquiry didn't prepare me for covering the Anita Cobby murder trial.

This tragic murder brought about, and rightly so, a healthy public respect for the work of police, journalists and the legal profession, professions which traditionally attract a fair amount of healthy Australian scepticism. The long hours I spent on the case ensured I came to know my professional media rivals, enjoying their company and even appreciating their work, but still keeping an eagle eye on them in case they scooped me. It also brought me in touch with police, solicitors, barristers and legal people away from the pressures of their work and when it was all said and done they were good company.

For me, it's imperative that this tragic story is preserved for our future generations to heed. That is why I have written this book. It is a story that could happen in any town at any time but it happened in modern-day Sydney. It is a story about human frailty and its shocking consequences. It is a story of courage and determination. But most of all it is a tribute to the ability of the human spirit to endure.

ON ANITA

"I could wish it was someone else's daughter but I can't, can I? They would then have to go through what we're going through." **Garry Lynch, Anita's father.**

"The greatest tribute to Anita was that she was a patient, caring nurse, for whom nothing was too much trouble. She had humility, with few knowing she was a former Miss Western Suburbs, but most of all her fellow nurses said she felt good about herself and had that wonderful gift for making others feel the same about themselves." **Dr John Raftos, President of the Board, Sydney Hospital.**

"She had no enemies in the world — God knows how something like this could have happened." **Grace Lynch, Anita's mother.**

"There was so much more to her than good looks. She had an inner goodness that came out in her eyes and smile. I just want to remember her the way she was . . . the most beautiful thing in the world." **Anita's husband, John Cobby.**

"Anita Cobby has now gone on to a bizarre kind of martyrdom. For few murder cases here have so inflamed the passion of the populace as the butchery of a girl who was, in the words of the police officer who led the investigation, in the wrong place at the wrong time." **Frank Crook, senior columnist, The Sun.**

Chapter 1

The heart of Sydney is the spectacular and cosmopolitan city on the harbour. But if its bridge, Opera House, shops, Rocks and Kings Cross areas, restaurants and nightlife comprise the heart of Sydney, then the sprawling suburbs to the west are its muscles, its arteries, its backbone.

Most Sydneysiders live in the western suburbs, where the population is booming. It's here you'll find battlers, self-styled fair dinkum Aussies, true-blue mates. There are more factories in the west than in any other area of Sydney, and more small businesses and schools. The west is Sydney's biggest nursery for the next generation of young Australians.

As in all burgeoning areas in modern Australia, crime, too, is on the increase in the western suburbs. Of specific concern to police and citizens is that many of the social ills there involve the young: truancy, drug and alcohol abuse, house-breaking, car theft, assault, rape. Garry and Grace Lynch and their daughters Anita and Kathryn lived in Blacktown, 41 kilometres west of the Sydney GPO, and next to Parramatta the largest city in the west. But in mid-1985, as the growing pains of their district intensified, Garry and Grace could reflect with pride that they had had no problems bringing up their daughters, not an ounce of trouble. Neither Anita nor Kathryn had roamed the streets, both had loved school, hated drugs and would never stay out all night. Now that both girls had married and moved out of home, the Lynchs were enjoying their retirement and looked forward to one day spoiling their grandchildren.

As a graphic artist with the Navy, Garry Lynch had worked hard all his life to provide for his family. He'd loved his work but now he relished the freedom to jump in the little camper van he and Grace had invested in and head to Lightning Ridge in the central north of NSW where they had an opal claim. Maybe one day they would strike it lucky.

A lifetime habit of unashamedly basking in the sun for hours on end had left Garry Lynch's long, oval face furrowed and tanned. His wavy greying hair had receded a little, but tinted glasses, a legacy of his profession, could not conceal the delight in his eyes whenever he spoke of his family and their trips to the country.

Grace Lynch, a nursing sister, was a shy, gentle woman. She was known by her family and close friends as "Peg". She preferred to be called Grace by anyone else. Although officially retired, she still worked casual shifts at a local nursing home to make ends meet. It was a job she enjoyed and her patients loved her.

Grace was surprised when their eldest daughter, Anita, became a nurse as she had always hated the sight of blood. But Anita had a special rapport with the elderly and was wonderful with children. Grace was confident she would be a fine nurse.

It didn't seem all that long ago to Garry Lynch that he had first laid eyes on baby Anita at Sydney's Crown St Womens Hospital. "She had a little hook nose and dark skin and I wondered how we had ended up with this beautiful little thing," he said. Anita Lorraine Lynch, 7lb 4oz (3.29kg) with a puff of brown hair, was born in the last half hour of November 2, 1959.

Five years later another daughter was born. Kathryn was the last arrival in a loving family. Garry and Grace Lynch brought both babies home to their modest little fibro house in Sullivan Rd, Blacktown.

Anita enjoyed school from her first day at nearby Walters Rd Public School. Her mother remembered a neighbour's child starting school the following year and Anita stepping in to look after the distraught little girl. "Our neighbour's daughter was upset about having to leave her mother. Anita loved school and when she was asked to comfort the child she walked up to her and happily offered to look after her for the rest of the day."

Anita's kindness endeared her to others. It showed in everything she did, said her father. "She just got on well with everyone and she had a great love of animals. Both the girls did. If there was a sick bird or stray cat or dog, it would end up at our place."

The Lynchs encouraged their daughters to have interests outside of school and Anita joined the Girls Brigade. She enjoyed sports, particularly netball and softball. "Anita was a superb catcher and one year I bought her a catcher's mitt so we could practice in the backyard," Garry said. "She used to crack that ball back at me with a great force and we'd have a lot of fun out there in the yard."

One year when his daughters were still in primary school, Garry Lynch bought a small motor boat. He named it *Katani*, after Kathryn and Anita. The family would then plan their holidays around boating trips, often on the Nepean River. "We had some lovely times together," Grace said. "We shared everything as a family, our holidays, boating trips . . . the girls were wonderful friends. Watching them grow up and develop was a happy time for us."

Like so many families, the Lynchs recorded many of these simple moments with a home video camera. Anita, as a toddler, holding onto her mother's hands walking across a small bridge, a smiling Anita clutching a doll, with her proud Dad, patting a cat, and in another sequence swinging around and around a Hill's Hoist clothes line. A family favourite shows Anita holding her mother's hand and skipping along in the snow which she picks up and eats. How they loved that film.

Anita's teenage years were happy and uncomplicated. She fretted about blemishes on her face as most girls do and was careful about her diet. She went through a stage of not liking her thick, wavy hair. At one stage she tried to have it straightened, without success "and then finally accepted it the way it was," said Grace Lynch. Anita's luxuriant hair was so thick she had to groom it with a wide-combed brush.

As she grew older, Anita enjoyed jogging and came to be fond of the outdoors. Like her father, she was a sun worshipper. "She really loved the beach and would lie in the sun every chance she could. She'd sunbake in the backyard sometimes before she started work at the hospital. She had lovely olive skin that would tan up well," Garry Lynch said.

Garry Lynch recalls with amusement Anita's interest in music. "She was good at music and played the electronic organ beautifully, but then she was introduced to the transistor radio and she never played another note," he said. "Like most teenagers she had a preference for heavy rock bands at first. The old house used to jump a bit, but then she went through her Carole King and Carly Simon stage and it was much quieter." She also enjoyed the ballads of Elton John and some of the classical records her father had at home.

Anita had a good eye for art. It was a family trait. After some coaching by her father she found she liked drawing and took art as a subject in her Higher School Certificate. Her aunt Cecelie was an accomplished water colour artist.

At school, Anita was studious and popular with her peers. She was elected a prefect while she completed her Higher School Certificate at Evans High in Blacktown. Towards the end of her schooling she had a steady boyfriend who was the son of a family friend, Anne Farmer. They were more like best mates, doing everything together, including hours of study.

Undecided about a career after school, Anita took her first job in an office but soon realised office work was not for her. Her beauty, her poise and personality were now starting to shine through as she gained confidence out in the world.

It was Anne Farmer who persuaded Anita to enter the Miss Australia Quest to raise money for the Spastic Centre, because she knew of Anita's love for children. "We were walking through Westfield Shopping Centre when we saw a sign for the Quest," Anne Farmer said. "I thought it would do Anita the world of good to enter something like that because she was still very shy." The Lynchs raised more than $10,000, mainly by selling raffle tickets at their local shopping centre. Garry remembered the day they went to see the Spastic Centre kids at Allambie Heights. "A wheelchair-bound boy painstakingly tapped out a message for her on his computer using a stick attached to his head. She patiently waited until he had finished and it read: 'Gee, I could go for you.' Her personality just seemed to catch people like that."

The Quest thrust her into the limelight and she was photographed having afternoon tea with the then NSW Premier Neville Wran and leader of the State Opposition, Nick Greiner, with leading jockey Malcolm Johnston, and the captain of the *Fairstar* cruise liner. Anita won the Miss Western Suburbs Charity Queen title and was photographed, with a petite tiara perched on her head, accepting the award from the then State Attorney-General Frank Walker. By now, she had a wide circle of friends. Her appealing personality unfailingly endeared her to people. Anne Farmer remembered her saying she could get on with anybody. "She just had a lovely way with people. I had an old aunt who adored Anita. They would sit and talk for hours. She just had this wonderful warmth inside that would put people at ease. Everyone who came in contact with her would feel it," she said. "She had friends everywhere she went," remembered Grace Lynch.

Next Anita took up modelling for the Westfield shopping centre chain. Tall and willowy, with a dazzling smile and large eyes, success was assured. During the Quest, organisers had made her straighten her thick, corkscrew curls with a perm. "She didn't seem to mind the change," said Anne Farmer. "It was shoulder length then and turned under and the style looked attractive on her. She always had the most beautiful hair."

Anita emerged a new person from the Quest and her modelling days. Said Garry, "It put that final polish on her and gave her confidence and I suddenly realised what a beautiful young woman she was. This is not just a proud father talking here. She had natural beauty and didn't need to wear makeup. But she did use a bit of lipstick or eyeshadow when she was going out."

Modelling, however, demanded much of her and eventually Anita gave it away. The heavy makeup and the shallow lifestyle was not her style. Anita was too spontaneous and ingenuous to take the glittery milieu of modelling seriously. Aged 20, Anita applied to enter both the police force and nursing, sending the applications off together. The nursing details arrived back first and Anita began her training at Sydney Hospital. The family was taken aback. "It was one of the greatest surprises of my life when she went into training and became a sister," said her mother. "I had said to her once when she was younger, 'Why don't you try nursing?' and she had said, 'Yuk, blood, bedpans.' I was delighted because I thought she had an inner quality that would be wonderful in that field." Garry said he was proud when she graduated and moved into the specialised field of micro-surgery. "I think it is one of the worst sections of nursing that a young mind can be subjected to. It is pretty horrific, all that mutilation, but she was a superb sister."

Chapter 2

John Travers was only 13 when he was charged with possessing marijuana and a bong. His mate Michael Murdoch was actually smoking the drug when Murdoch's mother Rose caught them at her house. Travers and Murdoch were the same age and lived in the same street in a Housing Commission estate in Mount Druitt, near Blacktown. They were also enrolled at the same school, not that they attended often. Rose Murdoch told Travers' mother Sharon about the marijuana incident and she was hopping mad. "I grabbed John by the scruff of the neck and dragged him down the police station and had him charged," she said. Murdoch was charged too.

The 12-month probation on the marijuana charge, handed out in the Cobham Childrens Court in December, 1980, didn't bother Travers. He figured he had just been unlucky, especially since he'd been using the drug for a couple of years now. He remembered the first time he'd dragged on a joint a relative had given him. It made his head spin. The same relative introduced him to heroin a little later but Travers shied away because of his aversion to needles.

Travers was, however, more concerned about what would be in store for him when his old man found out about the drug charge. Violence.

As the eldest of the seven Travers children, John, or "Trawney" as he was nicknamed, was always expected to set a good example for the others. But his track record wasn't good. He attended Shalvey High for a short time but was expelled for "mucking up" and later was "asked to leave" Newman High at Greystanes, Travers later said. He hated school, rejected authority and, according to his mother, he was mixing with the wrong crowd. He'd spent a year at Boys Town, a juvenile detention centre, after his mother had him charged. He swore this was even worse than being at home because, he later said, "they flogged you heaps".

Back home, after Boys Town, life for Travers was unsettled and there were some huge rows with his father. By the time he was 14, he was drinking at least a bottle of whiskey a day and "Goons", flagons of moselle or muscat, while experimenting with a variety of drugs, including amphetamines. "He was drinking a lot of hot stuff — bombs, mixtures of things," said a friend who lived in the same street. He liked beer but preferred spirits and with the alcohol he became violent. "He was into dope no more than other kids our age then. We used to smoke it all the time because cigarettes were boring." Travers later told a prison psychiatrist he went to Boys Town because his mother "thought he (his father) was going to kill me."

John Travers and his father Ken, a bus driver, clashed constantly. According to Sharon Travers Ken didn't know how to handle his son and John didn't give a damn. The children defied and tormented their father. He often yelled at them, giving them backhanders and haranguing them to show his authority. But he was certainly no match for his wife. "He was very hen-pecked even though Sharon really didn't run a tight ship," said one neighbour. "But Sharon had a hold over them all. She would make the children fetch a stick if they had been naughty and they would bring it to her and then stand while she spanked them. She was too big to chase them. They just stood there and took it."

Sharon Travers weighed 127 kilos. She was too immobile to run the household. "It was really quite sad to see how that family lived," said a neighbour. "Sharon had many problems but the biggest one was herself and everyone suffered because of it. It was terrible to watch her deteriorate, growing heavier and sicker, because I had seen some photos of her and she had been a very attractive young woman."

Sharon was the second eldest of three boys and two girls. Her father deserted the family when she was just four years old. Her mother Loylene worked hard to care for them and later married again. In 1967 aged 17 Sharon married Ken Travers, eight years her senior, and in the same year gave birth to John. Lisa was born the following year, Peter in 1970, Christopher in 1971, Scott in 1973,

Jason in 1976 and Brock in 1977. One of Sharon Travers' friends remembered: "Growing up, the world was her apple and she was a woman who never wore the same blouse or skirt twice. She was a proud, pretty woman with a fantastic body and the prettiest blue eyes. But when she started to have children things began to go wrong. She had seven in quick succession and her body just didn't recover in between them. There was only 14 months between John and the next, Lisa. Doctors advised her after the second one not to have any more because she was having too many complications and her health was suffering. From then on, not being able to regain her figure, she let herself go and stopped taking care of herself. She grew huge and lost her self-esteem. She tried to get all sorts of medical help and was always on diets but would never stick to them."

Because she was so big, Sharon Travers found it difficult to move around. Most days she would sit in a large recliner chair watching TV, rarely moving. "She wouldn't, or couldn't, do the housework. Washing, cooking and hygiene or organising activities for the kids just weren't a priority," said another friend.

"She was so large she couldn't sit on the toilet seat. To even get to the toilet, she had to angle herself and back down the corridor, positioning herself over the seat. She often needed the help of the kids to guide her. She reached the point where she was too big to comfortably fit into some rooms in the house. And, because she couldn't bend, she couldn't bathe the kids. Consequently, the younger ones were often dirty with food and grime caked around their mouths. Sometimes they didn't have a bath for days."

Sharon often wouldn't wear knickers, according to one relative, because she couldn't find any big enough to fit her. She had some made but it was difficult putting them on, so she didn't. She couldn't buy clothes off the rack so these had to be made for her too.

The Travers family, having moved from Mt Druitt, struggled in a three-bedroom Housing Commission house at 5 Tich Place, Doonside, near Blacktown. It was a little weatherboard and brick house in the middle of a cul-de-sac. It looked just like all the others in the street, except for the ramp leading up to the front door. That was put in for the youngest child Brock's wheelchair. Born with spina bifida and now a paraplegic, he couldn't walk and needed special care.

Brock's ill health was a further strain on Sharon Travers who couldn't even care for herself, let alone her children. It wasn't that she didn't love them; she did. She just couldn't get out of her own way. At least the extra government allowance they received for Brock's disability supplemented the fortnightly single parent's pension on which the family survived after Ken left.

One aunt remembered how Sharon did nothing when doctors said they could help Brock walk with a series of operations (although they were done later). "I don't know if it was laziness through her obesity or what, but I was extremely angry when I found out nothing was done to help Brock," the relative said. "Brock was assessed by a specialist in the Youth and Community Services Department who said he was suitable to undergo a series of three operations and after-care that would allow him to walk. But these operations had to be performed before he reached a certain age, I think it was eight. He would have been financially covered for the operations and it would have changed his life, made it wonderful for him and easier for others. But he was denied the opportunity. It is so sad for him."

Because Brock couldn't stand up, he fared even worse than the others in the house. He had to rely on his brothers and sister to move him around. Brock could only reach the bottom part of the fridge and because Sharon didn't cook meals, he ate what he could reach. Brock eventually underwent surgery to strengthen his knees and ankles in March, 1987, which enabled him to walk with the aid of specially fitted boots and a walking frame.

The house was mostly untidy because it was up to the children to do the cleaning. Furnished with older style pieces, there was a wall unit in the loungeroom containing plaster 18th century figures and a few cheap glasses. There was an organ and an old lounge with ripped cushions and on the walls were portrait photographs of every child, a plastic crucifix and a print of a black brumby.

The cooking was Lisa's job. She was the only girl and carried a large responsibility. One neighbour remembered, "There were always dirty dishes in the sink and Lisa couldn't do everything. She had little schooling but she was extremely resilient. It wasn't her fault but she had this awesome responsibility to run the household thrust on her when she was only a young girl. She had to bear it the best way she could."

The family sometimes had to live without electricity when the bills wouldn't be paid and it would be cut off. Other times Sharon would just sit in the dark, unable to move to switch the lights on once the sun set.

Sharon was always being told her eldest boy, John, was a cute kid. He had her pretty pale blue eyes, fine fair hair and freckles. He had a dimple in his chin just like hers, too. All the Travers children may have been able to lead better lives given a more stable environment. "But they weren't encouraged to use that potential or to learn," said one of their aunts.

One neighbour in Mount Druitt, where they lived before going to Doonside, said: "The kids weren't brought up by the parents, they brought themselves up.

John Travers claimed later to a psychiatrist, in a report presented in court proceedings, that his father physically abused him. He told psychologist Dr Geoffrey Fox in February, 1987, about his father's alleged mistreatment of him when young.

In a report prepared for the NSW Supreme Court, Dr Fox wrote "his father was apparently a violent man and strongly given to sexual deviation. For example, he apparently encouraged his son to take girls under the house so that he could spy on their behaviours. However, he was particularly sensitive to any attention that John paid to his daughter, and apparently he would abuse John violently for anything he did suggesting a concern for his sister. For example, he told me that he would be belted just for putting the dummy back into his sister's mouth. His father was violent enough that whenever John tried to defy him, he would physically put him into a headlock and choke him until he fell unconscious. Naturally, I could not accept the above information on its face value but I feel sure there would be others who could confirm that this description was accurate or not . . ." When later questioned about her husband's behaviour, Sharon said she was unaware of anything like this happening, but added, "You don't know what happens when you are not there . . . it's possible . . ."

Psychiatrist Dr Hugh Jolly later said in an assessment of Travers, presented to court, that Travers' troubled childhood contributed to his anti-social behaviour. He attended many high schools but resented the discipline. He despised being told what to do by teachers. His attitude to authority was demonstrated by the fact that he never held a drivers licence despite having driven cars since he was 14 and never applied for a gun licence even though he'd used a gun for some time.

He was expelled from Doonside High School for exposing his penis to a teacher and was sent to a Catholic boys school, Newman High, at Greystanes. Here he stayed until Year 10. He wasn't good at schoolwork but in class, when he was there, he was quiet. He liked practical subjects and was good at technical drawing.

When Ken Travers left the family in 1981, and with his mother sick, John Travers was relied upon to pull the kids into line when they needed it. "He tried to take on the responsibility of looking after the kids, especially after Ken and I split," said Sharon Travers. "He tried to be firm, kind and supportive. It was difficult for him. It was a big responsibilty for John, but he would smack the younger kids if they needed it and pull them into line," she said. "It was probably better for John that his father wasn't around because they never got on from the day he was born. His father just expected too much from him. If John said 'White' his father would say 'Black'. It was like that all the time. He used to set the children against one another and say to Lisa, 'Hit John' and Lisa wouldn't want to do it and Ken would say, 'If you don't hit him, I'm going to hit him and you as well.' Then John would say to Lisa, 'For Crissakes hit me and get it over and done with.' Lisa would end up crying. Their father would get a kick out of seeing them at each other. Sometimes John would go to extremes to do the opposite of what his father had told him."

Sharon Travers once remarked that John was "such a good baby, I can't understand how he grew up into such a little monster". She said he was like any other normal small child. He liked to hide in cupboards, play football and ride his bike. "He was a good kid until he was about 10. After that he used to keep to himself and wouldn't talk to anyone. He was the type of kid who'd be sitting there not saying anything and you'd say, 'What's the matter?' and he'd say, 'Nothing', but half his finger would be hanging off."

Being the head of the house was difficult for John Travers because of his own lack of discipline. According to two young neighbours, there was an argument once between Travers and one of his younger brothers over the washing up. The young boy protested and Travers pulled the child's pants down and forced his thumb up his anus.

There was always a shortage of money in the Travers household because no-one worked. So, with no cash to buy groceries, John stole much of what he and his brothers and sister needed to live on. He started bringing home chickens and ducks for the family to eat. He'd steal them from people's backyards, fowl houses, small acreages or just catch them in the vast bushlands in the district. Sometimes he would sit on the back steps and shoot birds as they flew by. He'd kill them, feather them, clean them and then cook them.

By now Sharon Travers was spending more and more time in hospital. She had Cushings Syndrome, a disease causing the body's glands to produce an excess of steroids. As a result, she suffered from high blood pressure, diabetes, a florid complexion, her skin would stretch, her kidneys would regularly fail and she had a cough that sounded like a whooping cough, often making her speak in a low, husky voice. It was a condition that was treatable, however, because of her inability to help herself, it became progressively worse. Each time Sharon Travers went to hospital, it was left to John to take over the running of the house while she was away. Often the children were sent to foster homes while she recovered.

Just two weeks after his 16th birthday, John Travers was put on 18 months probation and fined $70 for being an unlicensed driver, illegally using a motor vehicle and displaying P plates to mislead police. He needed the plates because he looked a lot younger than his years, even if the tattooed teardrop under his left eye starkly belied his baby face.

When Travers finished school the only job he stuck to for any length of time was at the Riverstone meatworks. But he soon lost interest. He mostly took on labouring jobs but preferred to collect the dole. He was now staying away from home more often and eventually went to live with his grandmother, Loylene, whom he adored. Loylene's death from cancer a few years later had a devastating effect on John Travers, according to his mother. "He blamed himself, although there was nothing he could have done. He just went off the rails and was drinking anything he could get his hands on and taking so many drugs. He just seemed to go downhill from there and there was no getting him back."

Travers' interest in stealing animals grew and the animals starting getting larger. He began to bring small lambs home. Next they reportedly became the objects of his sexual urges. His mates claimed to have seen him have intercourse with chickens, lambs, pigs and sheep at various times. It became his party trick, they claimed. John would have a lamb or pig to kill and cook for the party but, before he did, he would have intercourse with it and then cut its throat or belly.

One of those parties, in February, 1985, has gone down in Doonside folklore. It was Travers' 18th birthday. "He was drunk and stoned off his tits," Sharon Travers recalled later. "It was pretty late and he'd crashed out in his room. He often did that when he drank. I've seen him drink a bottle of scotch and I always knew he'd pass out, kaput, out to it every time, and you could never wake him. Well, it was one of those nights and before he crashed I kept saying, 'Tell the kids to go home.' He said, 'Just close the door and pull the cord out of the electric guitar and they'll leave.' That's what I did and went to bed. Next morning I find my yard's joined all the neighbours' yards. There were no palings on the fence. Not one. They burnt them to keep the fire going and then they threw what was left of the lamb on the spit into the next door neighbour's pool." She did, though, deny her son had had intercourse with animals. "I never had any hint about that at all," she said.

Chapter 3

Michael Murdoch, known as "Mick", was always hanging around with Travers. For a time, the pair was inseparable. Other youths would drift in and out of the group but Travers was always the kingpin. For a man who later told psychiatrists he had difficulty making friends, he had a strong hold over them all. They stole cars, got drunk, watched TV, rode the trains and carried guns and knives. The Wentworthville pool parlour was a favourite haunt and they were all good at a game of eight ball.

Young girls also frequented the pool parlour. Police say many were brutally forced to have sex with the youths and that Travers always led the charge. To him, and the others, girls were there for the taking. And they got away with it all because they were admired by their peers and protected by the unwritten law that Australians don't dob.

The Parramatta-to-Blacktown train line and beyond was also a hunting ground for girls. The stations were ideal spots for a gang to locate its prey. Raping girls was a benchmark for authority and power in their circle. Travers was proud of his reputation as a rapist around Blacktown. He loved to see women squirming and frightened. He enjoyed making them feel dirty.

Travers also loved bashing homosexual men. "Poofter-bashing" was entertainment. The gang would often rape their victims. "John would say how he'd go out looking for poofs and bash the hell out of them and then give them what they give others," said one of his aunts.

Ironically, years later, when asked by a police officer whether he was homosexual, Travers was indignant. He replied curtly that he wasn't. "There was much evidence that he did get with blokes but he considered himself not to be gay," the officer said.

Trawney Travers showed little respect for anything or anyone. But he was good with kids. He had plenty of practice at home with his little brothers. When he was in a happy mood he would spend time playing with them.

He also kept two white and tan bull terriers. One had a black patch over his eye. Their names were Arse and Cunt. "John was fairly rough with them. He would feed them, pat them, take them around with him, but also torment them," said an acquaintance.

Teenagers in the Doonside neighbourhood claimed that Travers on many occasions would scare people by eating small lizards. And once, one of Travers' mates, "Mad Dog", bit the head off a kitten. Sharon Travers later shrugged off her son's cruelty to animals, saying, "You know what 18-year-olds are like when they get together, biting the heads off kittens, swallowing gold fish . . . a lot of kids go through that stage."

She never considered her son's behaviour a cause for undue concern. "I knew John needed psychiatric help, but he wasn't what you'd call a deep-down disturbed boy. He didn't get violent, he'd withdraw. When he was a kid he'd often throw himself on the floor and say, 'That's it, time for the world to cut off.'"

Despite his violence towards women, Travers managed to have relationships. One was with a pretty, petite blonde teenager. "She was a cute little thing," remembered an aunt. "She spoke well, was neat and tidy and came from a reasonable home, all the things that he wasn't. John liked women he could dominate and tell what to do." Sharon Travers later said in a TV interview she considered John "had a normal attitude to girls".

John Travers had another girlfriend. It was an on-off relationship, convenient for sex. She claims she bore Travers' child, but Travers denies it. Together though, Travers and his girlfriend were on a road to destruction. She was a junkie. But he was also into many things she didn't like, such as aggression. Others were witchcraft and violent or supernatural movies. *The Texas Chainsaw Massacre* was a particular favourite. He loved seeing the victims in the movie being cut up. About this time he started carrying around a big hunting knife, replacing the flick knife he kept in his back pocket.

Mick Murdoch wasn't engrossed in witchcraft like Travers but he didn't mind the movies. The pair were blood brothers. They considered their friendship as strong as that of real flesh and blood siblings. When they were young, Murdoch and Travers cut their skin, then pressed the bleeding wounds together so their blood mixed. This crude ceremony meant they were bound for life and would never let each other down. Another initiation test for their brand of blood brotherhood was to have sex with the same woman simultaneously.

People often mistook the two for identical twins. Murdoch copied everything Travers did. He wore the same kind of flannelette shirt, had his hair cut the same way. Once, Travers shaved his head and Mick Murdoch did the same, much to his mother's horror. Murdoch had his ears pierced like Travers. Both had their nipples pierced and wore sleepers in them. At one time Travers wore a chain across his chest, hooked through the sleepers in his nipples. Even his mates thought that was going a little too far. Murdoch and Travers had many tattoos. Travers sported several obscene words and phrases on his penis. By the time they were 16 the pair were tattooing themselves with a battery-operated kit.

Sharon Travers said her son's genital tattoos were only known about after he admitted them to police. "He was being booked and the police asked whether he had any tattoos. He was in a rebellious enough mood to flop his old fella out on the table and say, 'Well here they are — here, here and here.'"

Travers' aunt said, "John and Mick lived for each other's friendship. If one was without the other they would get jumpy. The closeness was unusual but I don't think it was sexual."

Mick Murdoch, too, was from a single-parent family, his mother raising the children on her own. Like Sharon Travers, Rose Murdoch had many health problems, including having only one lung after an operation to remove the other infected one saved her life. A short, round-faced woman with a tight, greying frizzy perm, Rose Murdoch coughed as if she had bronchitis. This was the legacy of chain smoking with just one lung. She wore metal-framed glasses and thin, summer dresses, even in winter, keeping warm with just a cardigan. Mick Murdoch loved his mother, and everyone knew he was her favourite child.

But Rose Murdoch had never liked John Travers and hated his strong hold over her son. Rose was of the opinion that Travers was big trouble. She would regularly berate Mick over his bad behaviour, poor manners, thoughtlessness and laziness around the house, but Travers was the main bone of contention. So desperate was she to stop her son seeing Travers that she moved a few suburbs away from the Travers family at Mount Druitt.

Mick Murdoch was no stranger to the law. Back in February 1982, only one year into his two-year probation for the marijuana smoking conviction with Travers, he was back before the children's court, this time for being an accessory to a breaking, entering and stealing offence. Only two weeks after that he fronted again but this time at Minda Children's Court, after being picked up driving a car.

Chapter 4

It wasn't the first time Michael Murphy had been inside. This time he was doing eight years for breaking, entering, stealing and larceny. The time before he had been sentenced to 10 years for his part in an armed robbery.

He felt the imprisonment this time was unfair, especially as he had not been armed with a weapon himself and he'd even tried to restrain one of his fellow robbers from attacking someone during the raid. His job had been to wait outside while the others carried out the robbery. One had been armed with a pick handle. But the robbery went wrong, the law held Murphy as guilty as the rest and there he was again, behind bars. By late 1985, he had spent a lot of his 29 years in gaol.

If anything, gaol had slowed Mick Murphy down. Once, he had closely cropped hair and an earring that made him look, with his thick dark eyebrows and dark eyes, like a pirate. His arms were covered in tattoos, with "Nan" above the left elbow, "Kelley" and a spider web. Other names have been blotted out. On his right forearm, a tattoo shows an Andy Capp-type character urinating and the word "Sharpies" underneath. He was a member of a so-called Sharpies gang in the '70s. The gang was into heavy metal rock and fighting. Their main targets were the rival surfie and bikie gangs that crossed their path at any of the haunts the Sharpies frequented. Places like the Town Hall Hotel in the city or the Menzies' Cellar and games halls like Playland in Pitt Street.

The Sharpies spent a lot of time at a Christian outreach centre, Club 200, run in the '70s by Wesley evangelist and now prominent politician the Rev Fred Nile. Nile remembered the gangs used to congregate in the church's city headquarters "because they had nowhere else to go" but that the aggression between the gangs was intense. One weekend, said Nile, Sharpies were responsible for smashing all the windows in shops in the Wesley Arcade. The windows were kicked in one weekend during a wild brawl. Nile himself was once beaten up.

Nile remembered the Murphy family well. "They seemed to have a continuous run of problems and I was often in court giving character references for them," he said.

Mick Murphy's look had mellowed with age and longer hair. His collar-length, regular prison cut made him look more like his brothers. At first glance Mick Murphy could be just another Saturday afternoon drinker at any hotel, having a punt on the horses.

Mick is the eldest of the nine children born to Dulcie and Leslie Murphy. The family spent its early years in small, rented federation homes in Erskineville in the inner city. They weren't well educated but the father was a hard worker. He held down two jobs. During the week he worked at the old Central Tooheys brewery and on weekends he operated a small fishing trawler to help supplement the family's income. One of the boys remembered him as "a tough old man, hard to get on with and he always thought he was right even if he wasn't. It was easier to leave him alone than to try to talk to him".

Later, when the brewery closed and the family moved out west he got a job working the door at the large Blacktown Workers Club.

Dulcie was strict on the kids, especially when it came to manners, but as they grew older and there were so many of them they became harder to control. Their father, though, was stern with all of them.

Mick Murphy remembered an occasion when he was speaking on the phone and his brother was "being a smart-arse, so I just put the phone down, went straight over there, opened up the sliding door and gave it to him. He'd been mouthing off and paying out too much and I'd had enough of him."

People often joked that the Murphys had so many children that they ran out of names. So when another boy was born they recycled Michael Patrick's name and called the baby Patrick Michael.

These were tough times for a big family and the Murphy kids were often sent out to collect glass soft drink bottles which earned a penny if they were returned to the storekeeper. "None of our families were rich but the Murphys had so many kids that they never seemed to have anything much."

When Mick was about 12 his mother decided she couldn't care for him any longer and sent him to live with his grandparents at Little Bay near La Perouse on Botany Bay. Little Bay shared a border with the Long Bay Gaol complex which Murphy would also come to regard as home. Living with his grandparents was pretty good. They adored him and when his grandmother and mother were both present, Murphy would call his nan "Mum" and his real mother "Dulcie". As far as Dulcie was concerned sending Mick away meant one less mouth to feed and one less mischief-maker to keep an eye on.

Mick Murphy spent a lot of time visiting his brothers and sisters. The younger kids, especially, regarded him as a protector and looked up to him. When he was away, that job fell to Gary. One schoolboy who lived a few streets away from the Murphys in Erskineville remembers the Murphys were always in trouble. "The Murphy brothers were always in blues," he said. "Not that we didn't get into scraps ourselves, but these kids were in 'em all the time. Causing most of 'em too. The younger ones would start them and if any of them were getting done over they'd always say they'd go and get their big brother Gary."

Gary Murphy, known as "Smurf", always looked like he could do with a feed and a good haircut. He was thinner than most of his brothers and his hair was shoulder length and straggly, parted at one side. It was lighter than Mick's and later when it was cut short you could see his thick eyebrows, a characteristic of the Murphy boys.

The family was well known in the Erskineville neighbourhood but not for the right reasons. One young paperboy likened the Murphy house in Binning St, to the Munsters', the creaky, dilapidated home of the popular TV characters. "The house was a bit rundown and there was always things lying around out the front — bits of old furniture, rubbish, it wasn't looked after. And the old girl was always yelling at the kids. There was always fights and screaming from there as the kids got a hiding. I was even too scared to walk past so I used to cross the road and walk around. Often, things would come flying out the door or windows during a fight. Everyone else in the neighbourhood did the same."

The family moved frequently as the leases on their rented homes weren't renewed. One of the places they stayed the longest was in a terrace house in Lilyfield Rd, Rozelle, across the road from the train goods yard near White Bay. This was before they were approved by the Housing Commission for a bigger house at Delaney Drive, Doonside.

It was here, at Rozelle, that the boys took a keen interest in the local rugby league side, Balmain. The Balmain Leagues Club was less than a kilometre away on Victoria Rd and the team's home ground was Leichhardt Oval, another two kilometres away. All the boys were encouraged to take up sport and were taught to box by their father, a one-time amateur boxer. As well, the boys played sports organised by their local Police Boys Club but never stuck at any game for long.

Mick's first brush with the law was as a 17-year-old caught pinching a car in 1970. Three weeks later he was charged with a second car stealing offence and this time spent 12 months at a children's institution. All the Murphy boys had police records by the beginning of 1986 except for the youngest, Peter. At 16, one of them was serving time for armed robbery.

Mick didn't stick at school and got a job as a car detailer for a car yard along "auto alley" on Parramatta Rd. He worked his way up and became a car salesman. After that, as brother Pat put it, "He went thieving" and another brother said while the other Murphy boys were just "in and out" of gaol, "Michael's got into the most trouble."

Gary Murphy is five years younger than Mick. His life of crime was first documented at the age of 14 when he was caught stealing. Two years later he was handed over to the Social Welfare Department after convictions for larceny of a motor vehicle and driving without a licence. He escaped from a juvenile home and took off to Victoria where he was caught and handed back to NSW authorities.

Due to a speech problem caused by a hearing defect, he was sent to Enmore High where they had a slow learners class but his poor attendance contributed to his early departure from school. His first job was working for Rozelle builder Claude Marocco, who never had any trouble with Gary Murphy at all. In fact he was "a good kid" who "always had a smile on his face. He would do his work when asked". Murphy had many tattoos, most on his arms. They included "Home Made", the initials G.M., a spider web on one elbow, a heart and chains around his wrists and the names of his two sons to a former girlfriend.

But Gary Murphy's fascination with cars often got him into trouble. He liked to work on them and do them up and he was good with engines, even as a youngster. He was always on the lookout for cheap, easy-to-come-by, vehicles and parts. His mates, too, always brought their cars to Gary to be fixed or changed in some way to avoid detection if hot. In July, 1975, at Kurri Kurri he was charged by warrant for the theft of a motor vehicle and was committed to an institution for nine months.

Gary Murphy's police record is well documented:

Lidcombe Petty Sessions: April 12, 1976. Break, enter and steal. Suspended self recognisance. $100 good behaviour bond.

Lidcombe Petty Sessions: May 5, 1977. Fail to comply with those conditions on recognisance. Six months hard labour.

Sydney District Court: September 6, 1977. Five charges of break, enter and steal. Six months hard labour on each to be served concurrent with next sentence. Break, enter and steal with intent. 18 months hard labour to commence at expiration of current sentence.

Penrith District Court: February 2, 1978. Escape lawful custody. Three months hard labour to commence at end of current sentence.

Parramatta District Court: July 24, 1979. Two charges of larceny of a motor vehicle. Two years gaol on each, concurrent.

Blacktown Petty Sessions: January 12, 1981. Goods in custody, unlawfully possess a registration label, unregistered and uninsured motor vehicle, unaccompanied learner. Total fines of $450 or 20 days hard labour.

Blacktown Petty Sessions: October 19, 1981. Unlicensed driver, unregistered and uninsured motor vehicle. Fined total $300 or 12 days hard labour.

Parramatta Petty Sessions: May 3, 1984. Steal a motor vehicle. Two hundred hours community service or 24 days hard labour.

Blacktown Petty Sessions: March 27, 1984. Goods in custody, resist arrest, unregistered and uninsured motor vehicle and plates calculated to deceive. Fined total of $600 or 27 days hard labour.

Generally, Gary Murphy was regarded as a likeable fellow, always popular with the women because of his boyish, almost shy smile and his inability to turn a girl down. At any given time he'd have at least three girlfriends. One neighbour remembered a time when Gary Murphy was seeing every girl in his street, including her daughter. "I don't know what they saw in him. But I must say he always treated the girls nicely." One time Dulcie Murphy was so sick of answering the telephone to take messages for Gary from his girlfriends, she had it disconnected. Later, when he was in prison, women would fight over who could take the allocated visits.

But Gary Murphy did have a problem with his temper. He had a short fuse which when it blew usually caused a fight, especially after he'd been drinking or smoking dope. His first reaction was to solve a dispute with a punch and he frequently found himself in fights. He was barred for life from the Rooty Hill RSL after brawling there and once had his jaw broken in another pub fight.

Younger brother Les was a tough little nut. The size of a jockey, he had a cyclonic temper. He was cocky too. Only two days before his 10th birthday Les appeared at Ashfield Childrens Court on a break, enter and steal charge and was given three years probation. But that did nothing to deter him and less than a year later he was at Ashfield Court again on the same charges. This time he was given 12 months probation but 10 months later in Windsor Court he was committed to an institution after being convicted of car stealing.

His life of crime was well under way. Some 11 months later he came before the Yasmar Childrens Court on another break, enter and steal charge and again he was sentenced to an institution. A year after that he was back there again after being convicted of illegally using a motor vehicle. By then he was four months short of his 14th birthday.

So it continued. Nine months later Les Murphy came before Yasmar Childrens Court on two charges of taking and stealing a motor vehicle. On one of these he was committed again to an institution and received a suspended self recognisance of $100. He was also charged with being a neglected child and was given 18 months probation on both the remaining charges. He was enrolled at Cleveland Street High School in inner Sydney but did not attend regularly because he did not like to study.

The following records show only the times he was convicted of crimes. There were many more occasions when he was in trouble with police:

Yasmar Childrens Court: August 10, 1978. Two charges of stealing. Fined $1200 or four days detention.

Yasmar Childrens Court: January 24, 1979. Charged with being carried in conveyance (passenger in stolen car). Fined $100 or four days detention.

Albion Street Childrens Court: December 7, 1979. Possess lysergic (an illegal drug). Twelve months probation.

Wauchope Petty Sessions: January 12, 1982. Four charges of stealing. Suspended self recognisance of $500 good behaviour bond and fined $750.

The following year in the Central Criminal Court Murphy appeared on two sexual intercourse without consent charges. On each he was given three years gaol to be served concurrently. Two months later he was sentenced to 12 months hard labour for being a passenger in a stolen car.

Les Murphy loved sideshows and the carnival way of life. He sometimes picked up work with a circus but more often liked stalking the midway in search of kicks. He spent a lot of time in pinball parlours and pool rooms too. Once, in Erskineville, police came running into a pinball parlour and yelled, "Has anyone seen Les Murphy?" None of the players gave him up. Murphy put his head down and kept playing until the police departed.

The brothers often caught up with each other in juvenile institutions and, later, in gaols as they served their time.

Chapter 5

John Travers had raped women many times before, his victims, police are certain, numbered more than one dozen, but now was the first time he was worried. He'd grabbed a girl near the Toongabbie railway station, two suburbs from Blacktown, heading back to Parramatta. She had struggled and when she cried he had bashed her. And then he'd forced her to have sex. Travers was certain she had had a good look at his tear drop tattoo and would be able to identify him. He had to get away. He decided to lie low in Western Australia until the heat died down.

Without much organisation, Travers left Sydney with a friend in a black Falcon utility, travelling down the coast to Melbourne, then across to Adelaide and on to Port Lincoln on the Eyre Peninsula, tip of the Great Australian Bight. Two more mates went too, following in a white Falcon utility.

At Port Lincoln, Travers and his gang raped again. This time the girl put up a fierce struggle but "they did horrid things to her", according to Travers' "aunt", his uncle's girlfriend, to whom he recounted the details later. The victim knew they were from out of town and had seen their faces. Travers panicked and fled back home to Sydney, leaving the utility behind because he feared he'd be picked up in it.

Travers went straight to the home of his uncle in Wentworthville. The uncle and his girlfriend were shocked to see him back so soon. And where was the utility? He didn't explain why he had left Port Lincoln in a hurry. John was often irrational, they thought. But as soon as he was home Travers became worried about the vehicle. "He begged us to go to get his car, he'd left it in the middle of somewhere over there," said the uncle's girlfriend. "I know it sounds mad but we jumped in the car and drove him all the way back to

Port Lincoln in 26 hours, dropped him off, turned around and came home. We didn't know what had happened there or it would have been different. If only we had known a lot of things . . ." she pondered later.

Travers and his three friends, who had remained in South Australia, continued on from Port Lincoln to Western Australia after picking up the utility, finally stopping in the small coastal tourist town of Mandurah, 75 kilometres south of Perth. It was a pretty little fishing village. Stan Szostak first went to Mandurah in 1983 to work at the small police station. He was the senior of the two detectives there. They worked with a staff of 15 uniformed police. In winter the job was relatively easy but in summer, the tourist season, around 80,000 people would visit, outnumbering the locals 10 to one.

The gang found a house in Eldora Crescent, in nearby Falcon, to live in. They stole things to sell, to buy food and marijuana. The police soon became aware of their presence after the four had raised the suspicions of the locals, but it wasn't until one of Travers' gang was picked up for drink driving that they came under the direct notice of the police there. He was charged on July 20, 1985, and released.

Soon after Travers viciously raped and assaulted a youth. It was an attack that would take on chilling significance just a few months later. When details of the unbridled savagery inflicted on an innocent Sydney nurse came to light, Travers' aunt, having been told repeatedly by Travers of the details of this assault in Western Australia, knew that John Travers was one person who may well be in a position to assist police with their enquiries.

While buying drugs one day, the gang met a 17-year-old homosexual living in a church-run refuge in Tuckey St, Mandurah, where Fenn Martin, a man of middle-age, was in charge. He did a good job counselling and caring for the 15 or so people under his roof. Some of them were fulltime boarders with nowhere else to go, others came part-time when they felt they needed the company or a change in their life. A proportion were drifters who stopped for a few nights on their way through town. Most had problems: involvement in drugs and/or prostitution, homelessness. Most had something to run from.

The four from the east coast started to call on the homosexual youth regularly. The loose friendship was based solely on drugs and sex.

In August they proposed a scheme where one of the gang, using a Polaroid camera, would photograph Travers having sex with the 17-year-old, then take the photos back to Sydney where Travers boasted they could be sold for $800 each. They told the youth he would get $400 for being in the photos. Travers was to receive the other half. The young man agreed to the scheme. He needed the money and he figured he may as well be paid for doing something he usually did for nothing. One of the gang took the photos of Travers and the youth while the other two waited in another room. Everything was fine. The four departed.

Later, however, they returned. This time they started pushing the 17-year-old boy around. They forced him out the back of the semi-detached house into a washroom. Two stood by the door and watched what happened next. The third held the camera. Travers took hold of the youth.

Travers was high on dope and alcohol. He grabbed the youth by the back of the neck, threw him hard against the washroom wall and pulled a large hunting knife from inside the front of his jeans. Travers pressed the knife hard against the young man to make him bend forward.

Travers ripped at his clothing, ordering him in a crazed voice to undo his jeans. He didn't loosen his grip on the youth's neck. The boy was frozen with fear. This wasn't part of the deal and, unlike the other times they'd had sex, this time Travers seemed out of control. In the short time he'd known Travers he'd seemed okay, full of schemes and a bit weird, but okay. Now Travers was freaking out.

Travers kept slamming the youth's head into the cement tub and against the wall. The boy screamed. Travers pressed the knife hard to his victim's throat and mounted the boy's back. He pushed the youth's thighs open with his knees and slid his own jeans down past his buttocks. Without warning, Travers clenched a fistful of hair and jerked the boy's head back. The boy began to cry. Travers pressed the knife in harder, under his earlobe now. Travers then raped the youth.

The young man said later he felt like he was about to pass out. Travers was in a frenzy. He pressed the knife harder, a sign for the youth to keep moving. The blade sent a trickle of hot fluid scurrying down the side of his neck. "All right, all right, I'll do anything but just don't hurt me," the young man gasped after realising the trickle of fluid was not sweat but his own blood.

As the youth realised that he may not survive this attack, Travers was grunting loudly and thrusting deeply, still holding the knife to his victim's face. The youth's knees ached and his back hurt from the clenched fist that Travers was pounding on him. The other three just stood and watched.

At last, Travers was done and slid off. The youth wanted to make a dash for the door but couldn't. He collapsed on the floor, still dazed. The others stood over him now. They had watched the whole thing and hadn't tried to help him. They hadn't seen Trawney use a knife like that before. He seemed over the edge, out of control, they thought. Travers grabbed the youth again and kicked him in the ribs. He warned him to keep his mouth shut or he would shut it permanently. Travers and one of the gang immediately left for Sydney. One caught the plane back while the other drove the ute.

Later that night Fenn Martin arrived at Mandurah police station. The battered youth was with him. Stan Szostak knew them both. He was concerned about the boy's condition. He took photos of the cuts and bruising across the boy's chest and neck then filled out the necessary reports. He now had names and descriptions of this Trawney Travers and his three mates. A medical examination showed the youth had also been cut around the anus. The youth was concerned he wouldn't see any of the money he'd been promised.

Before they left the station, Fenn pulled Szostak aside and told him there was a further problem. "The young man is suspected of having AIDS. He's had a test and finds out Friday what the result is."

Szostak went straight to the house in Eldora Crescent. There he found the two remaining gang members. They told him they'd tried to stop Travers and had taken no part in the rape. "I told them to pack their things and leave and when they caught up with their scrawny mate to tell him when he gets a chance, to see a doctor to have an AIDS test," said Szostak.

The pair were charged with using a false name, assault and stealing. They packed their belongings and left the state in the white utility. Later the homosexual youth wanted the charges dropped. He was concerned about reprisals. One experience with Travers was enough. Later that week the youth was told he had AIDS.

When Travers and his friend arrived back in Sydney in Spring, 1985, Travers showed his "aunt", the woman who lived with his mother's brother, a photo of his assault on the youth. She was dumbfounded. Travers told her about the rape in graphic detail, how he had seriously injured his victim. "His account scared the living daylights out of me," the woman who would become known as "Miss X" said later. "What they did to that poor boy was disgusting."

She felt guilty. This kind of thing simply shouldn't be allowed to happen. John mustn't get away with it. Someone had to be told. She claimed she called the Blacktown police station anonymously. "It was a dumb thing to do, I realise now, but I tried to have him picked up to teach him a lesson. Things were really getting out of hand," she said. "The police must have taken my call seriously because they sent around a car to check it out." But Travers outsmarted the police this time. He spotted them coming and made Mick Murdoch lie on the lounge and pretend he was Travers while Travers himself scooted out the back door and over the fence. Travers was good at hiding from police. Other times he'd conceal himself in the roof, scrambling through a hole where some of the roof tiles were loose.

Chapter 6

By 1982, Anita Lynch was settled and in love. While studying for her nurses certificate she had met John Cobby, a fellow nurse three years older than her. They spent hours together, and John helped Anita with her studies. He was an easy-going young man who loved horse racing. He held a trainer's license and also enjoyed surfing, skiing and watching sport. Their love of the outdoors was a common bond.

John Cobby had admired Anita at work for some months. He was not alone. Most other men at her new job had also noticed the dark-haired beauty. However, it took weeks for John to summon the courage to ask her out and he was stunned when she accepted his dinner invitation.

John took Anita to an inner-city Lebanese restaurant, The Prophet, in Cleveland St, Redfern, and it became their favourite haunt during the whirlwind 12-month courtship that followed. The pair worked together, studied together, went to the horse races, took bushwalks through the national parks and went to rock concerts around Sydney. They loved music and Anita was particularly fond of The Police and Talking Heads. They spent every available minute with each other. John's family adored her. Anita became good friends with John's sister, Gaynor.

The change in John Cobby was astounding. "John used to go out a lot with the boys," one friend said. "He was a knockabout bloke who liked a drink but after he met Anita he just wasn't interested. He spent all his time with her and we didn't see him out much after that."

Anita Lynch and John Cobby were married on March 27, 1982, in a church ceremony. Their reception was held in the backyard of John's grandmother's home in Arncliffe, a suburb south of

Sydney. It was typical of the pair. They didn't want any fuss. Just a handful of close friends and relatives attended and the wedding breakfast was prepared by the two families. "They were a happy couple, loving, laughing and always busy making plans," Grace Lynch said. "Anita was so happy and they were so in love."

After Anita finished her nursing studies two years later, the couple moved to a small farm they had rented at Boambee, just outside Coffs Harbour on the north coast of New South Wales, so John could pursue a horse training career. They bought two horses and trained them on the beach. The pair also worked at a private hospital in Coffs Harbour. A neighbour remembers Anita's special way with the horses, "although I got the impression she wasn't that keen on the racing side. She and John used to work hard on the property there but the horses didn't do much good for them."

Although they loved the beach, the country life, warm weather and each other's company, Anita wanted to travel. After three years of marriage the Cobbys were financially secure so they hastily arranged tickets and within a month had left on a 16-week tour of the world. Grace Lynch remembered Anita saying at the time, "If we don't go now we never will."

With no planning, they headed for the United States, where they hated New York but loved the west coast. From there they went to England and later travelled in Europe before returning overland through the Continent, coming back through Asia and spending their last two weeks on the beach in Bali.

Anita and John arrived home in July, 1985. Cold, wintry skies greeted them at the airport and their deep tans were in stark contrast to the pallour of other Sydneysiders. John soon found work at a nursing home along with a casual job at the Heart Foundation. He also went back to training horses. Anita found employment at her old hospital and they rented a house not far from John's family.

Within two months their marriage was all over. John and Anita separated. John moved in with his grandmother and Anita stayed on at the house. John said later, "The break-up came more or less out of the blue. Our overseas trip had brought us very close together . . . it made me very settled but Anita couldn't decide whether she wanted more travel or to settle down."

Soon after, Anita left the rented house and moved in

with a friend. "It was a difficult time for both of them," a mutual friend said of John and Anita's breakup. "Anita felt they were spending less and less time together and their interests were changing. She was upset about the split but John took it very badly and called her all the time. They were still good friends and I think he felt they would get back together."

Anita threw herself into her work and spent a lot of time with her friends and colleagues. John resigned from the Heart Foundation and sold his horses in the hope of having more time to spend with his wife. "We were very sad about the breakup but we told them we loved them both," Grace Lynch said.

The Christmas of 1985 was the first one Grace and Garry had spent without both their girls living at home. By now Anita's sister Kathryn and her childhood sweetheart Ray Eedens had married and were living just a few suburbs away from the Lynchs. Grace and Garry were therefore pleased when Anita returned home in the New Year to live in her old room in the little house at Blacktown.

Chapter 7

Rose Murdoch was too concerned about the behaviour of her sons to worry about Christmas that year. She had heard John Travers and her son Mick boasting of the Mandurah attack many times now and it still alarmed her. John Travers had always bothered her and she hated the way he influenced Mick who just had to be with Travers all the time. She was never sure of Travers. She said he had that empty gaze in his eyes, like he was looking right through you.

Finally, Rose Murdoch decided to put a stop to the friendship. She reported the Mandurah attack to Blacktown police station. It is recorded on the station's occurrence pad as a "telephone message at 4pm on December 22, 1985" when Mrs Rose Murdoch complained about her son Michael's association with John Travers. She mentioned the Mandurah attack but said she wasn't sure of the details and thought Travers may have been charged over there. The incident was noted and passed on to the Blacktown Detectives Office and logged in the crime intelligence file, a dossier of local identities, their movements, friends and associates, relatives, aliases and hangouts.

Across the Sydney suburbs in Silverwater Gaol Mick Murphy had all the time in the world to think about Christmas. Not that it meant much to him because he hadn't spent a Christmas outside for years, but given a choice he would rather be home with his family watching his 10-year-old daughter open her presents than in Silverwater behind bars.

The day after Boxing Day, 1985, Murphy was gone. Out the gate. He didn't mean to walk, in fact he had escaped a few times before and had always come back, but this time he blamed a prison mate.

Murphy and his mate allegedly told police later they had organised to meet a man to score some drugs but when they arrived at the pre-arranged meeting spot the fellow wasn't there. The mate faltered with this taste of freedom and didn't want to return but Murphy talked him into going back. On their return, they were spotted by a guard. The mate decided then to run for it and Murphy said he followed.

He went to the home of a woman who was friendly with his mother and stayed there for two weeks. His brother Gary came to see him a few times and took him out. But Gary hadn't been long out of gaol himself and both were broke. Gary took him to meet Ray Paterson, a man Gary had lived with for some years.

The Patersons lived in a corner house in Tivoli Place, Doonside, in a leafy Housing Commission estate. Nearly all the houses in this area had been built by the Housing Commission. Ray Paterson worked part-time removing furniture and his wife Judy looked after their three girls. Gary Murphy spent a lot of time working on his cars in their yard, because he didn't have a place of his own.

Not far from there was the Travers' house, where Les Murphy now lived with John Travers' sister Lisa in the caravan in their backyard. In a coincidence, at one time the Murphy family had lived at 7 Tivoli Place.

For the next few weeks the fugitive Mick Murphy moved around, staying here and there with friends and relatives. He went out with his brothers, once even to a party. He made new friends. One's name was John Travers.

Chapter 8

It was Sunday, February 2, 1986. At the end of their shifts Lyn Bradshaw and Anita Cobby sat down for the first time that day, in the waiting room with a cool drink in their hands. Weekends in the surgical area of Ward 14, Intensive Care Ward, were usually quieter than the rest of the week. At Sydney Hospital that day there was no surgery booked and doctors didn't do rounds, but usually there were a lot more visitors than during the week. Typically the Sunday started with helping patients with their breakfasts, changing bed linen, bathing and showering patients, checking dressings, handing out medication and taking temperatures, pulses and blood pressure. After morning tea, with another nurse on the medical end of the ward, Anita helped patients with their lunches and again there was another round of dispensing medication and taking pulses, temperature and blood pressure. The end of the shift was usually spent writing up reports before preparing for the next shift to take over.

Lyn Bradshaw remembered how that morning one of the patients had wolf-whistled Anita in the ward. "She turned around and glared at him and said: 'Wolf whistles are for dogs!'"

After chatting for a while the pair were joined by Elaine Bray. The three girls had known each other for about five years, since their training days together. The day before they had decided to go to a Lebanese restaurant for dinner and now they sat around killing time until the restaurant opened. During the afternoon Anita had taken a call from John. He was at the beach surfing, and they spoke for several minutes before Anita rejoined her friends. One of the girls remembered she appeared a bit distracted after the call.

The three friends chatted as they changed into their street clothes. Anita rolled up her white uniform and put it in her large tote bag. At 5.30pm they left. It had been a hot day, 38.5 degrees. The breeze outside was still warm. Elaine took her car and Anita went with Lyn. They met up at the entrance to Azars Lebanese restaurant in Elizabeth Street, Redfern, not far away.

There was nothing unusual about the dinner. The girls sat making plans to go to Perth together at the end of the year. Anita had been to Perth and liked it. Lyn was going there for a holiday shortly and Elaine would transfer over. Fanciful really, but they talked about living like millionaires and having a great time, plans they knew they would never keep. Lyn and Anita also discussed sharing a flat together when Lyn's lease ran out on her current flat in another month's time.

The three women shared two bottles of wine and left the restaurant at around 8.30pm. Anita needed a lift to Central railway station to catch a train back to Blacktown and despite offers from both girls for her to stay the night in town with them, she wanted to get home.

Lyn dropped Anita off in Eddy Avenue, the main entrance to catch the suburban trains. As Anita stepped out of the car, she turned around and said, "See you tomorrow."

Chapter 9

It was just before midnight. Garry Lynch was sitting on the edge of his bed. He had half expected a call from his daughter Anita wanting to be picked up from Blacktown railway station. She'd mentioned earlier in the day she would probably go to dinner with a few girls from work and be home around 10pm. But now it was late so she'd obviously decided to stay the night with one of her friends.

Garry gazed out of his bedroom window, fascinated by the cloud formations in the sky. The night was bright, lit by a clear moon, and warm. The clouds were rolling into each other, changing shape, twisting and turning, sparking his imagination. Then, recalled Garry, "One of the clouds turned into the most evil face I could ever imagine." The chilling shape stayed almost the same for some time, highlighted by the moon. It was eerie but he stared it out. Then the night wind turned the evil face into something else and it rolled away.

Grace Lynch rose at 6.15am on Monday to get ready for work. She peeped around the door of Anita's room and saw she hadn't come home during the night. She mentioned this to her husband but they weren't concerned. Anita often stayed over with friends if she had an early shift the next day.

Garry was up too, ready to drive his wife to work in time to start her 7am shift. He collected the newspaper on his way back home and ate breakfast in the sun on the back porch, skimming the headlines. Later he pottered around the house. He was enjoying the summer's warmth. Even though it was a bit cloudy it was still a lovely day. Summer was his favourite time of the year and he cherished the feel of the sun beating down on his skin.

During the afternoon the telephone interrupted his daydreams on the back verandah. He picked it up. "Hello Mr Lynch, this is Sister Jolly from Sydney Hospital calling, is Anita there please?"

"No, she isn't," Garry replied. "I think she must have stayed over with friends last night because she didn't come home."

"She was due to start at 1.30 today and we haven't heard from her. I don't want to alarm you, Mr Lynch, but I have checked with Elaine and Lyn and they are concerned as well. Lyn dropped her off at Central last night."

The call puzzled Garry. He phoned his wife to see if she had heard from Anita during the day. She hadn't. He called Sister Jolly back. She'd heard nothing more.

Lyn Bradshaw had been surprised at 2pm when Anita was late for work. "She was always reliable and almost totally dependent on public transport so she would allow herself plenty of time to get where she had to be. She would always ring even if she was just a few minutes late."

When there was still no word by 3pm Lyn Bradshaw became worried. Sister Jolly checked and confirmed there had been no sick call taken for Anita. She called Garry Lynch again. They decided he should report his daughter missing to Blacktown police.

Chapter 10

Blacktown police station is usually a hive of activity. There are few quiet days. As one of the central stations in the western suburbs, Blacktown has a large staff of uniformed police and a sizeable detective force. It's nothing special to look at. It is a building that echoes the 1950s, an odd shape borne out of being built in different stages around a courtyard. It is made of white brick, has two storeys, tinted windows and wood panelling at the entrance. It backs onto the railway line.

It was 6.30pm and still light when Garry Lynch walked into Blacktown police station. He told the young constable on duty he wanted to report a missing person. His daughter. The constable was sympathetic to the elderly gentleman's plight. He listened while Garry recounted the details of the phone call from her work. He stressed she was reliable, had never been in trouble and that she would usually ring if she was going to be late. To the young policeman it sounded all too familiar.

"Are you sure she hasn't stopped off at a friend's place?" he asked. Garry shook his head. The constable studied the photograph the old man had brought with him. He looked back at the father. Garry's face was lined with worry and his voice was faltering. His deep breaths gave away his panic. "A new boyfriend perhaps?" suggested the policeman. It had happened before. Parents come in distraught and report their daughter missing then phone later to say she has arrived home after a big night out.

"No, this isn't like Anita. She *is* reliable," Garry insisted.

The constable believed him. There was something about this man's story that made him feel uneasy. He checked with Const Paul Davies, also on duty that night. He went back to the counter. "We don't usually make out a missing person report until 24 hours after the person has been missing," he explained, "but I'll take down all the details now anyway."

He looked at the face of the girl in the photograph again, smiling under a mop of wavy dark hair. She looked familiar, he thought, as he put a piece of paper in his typewriter. Yes, he knew her. He told Garry he had attended the same high school as Anita. She was a few years ahead of him but he remembered her as a nice girl.

Garry Lynch looked at the report. The constable had typed his name there. "Const Murphy." It was a surname that would haunt him for the rest of his life.

The missing person report recorded that Anita Lorraine Cobby, maiden name Lynch, was "last seen at 9.00pm 2/2/86 walking into the entrance of Central railway station" and stated that she was on her way to her home address. "Fail to return home and fail to report for duty at the Sydney Hospital at 1.30pm 3/2/86 and failed to telephone off sick."

It also recorded that Anita Cobby was 175cm tall, of thin build with hazel eyes, black hair and olive complexion and her "racial appearance" was "white". In his panic, Mr Lynch recorded his daughter's age as 25 and her year of birth as 1960, a year after she was actually born. The report went on: "Last seen waring (sic) red and white stripes, straight leg jeans, white singlet top with 3 buttons at the neck. Black belt, brown/black moccosin (sic) type shoes, black large handbag with brown trim. Reason for Enquiry: Concern for welfare."

Next day dawned bright and sunny, but not for the Lynchs. Their other daughter Kathryn arrived early with her husband Ray to see if there had been any news of Anita. Although Kathryn was five years younger than Anita, the sisters were very close. They shared the same fine, creamy skin which tended to be olive in the summer months and the same dark, almost doe-like eyes. However, Kathryn's features were finer and she wore her hair short and streaked honey blonde. Like Anita, one eye was slightly lighter in shade than the other, which added to the beauty of the girls.

A family call to the Blacktown police station shed no new light on the disappearance. John Cobby called the Lynchs. He, too, had heard nothing. He was beside himself. The night before, Monday night, he'd been dining at Prophet's, his and Anita's favourite restaurant, with his father. His mother had called the restaurant to say Anita hadn't arrived home on Sunday night and no-one had heard from her. He couldn't finish his meal. He'd left immediately for the Lynchs' home. While he was there he called all her friends and the local hospitals in case she'd been injured, and then hours later, with no word, he left. This was the night he and Anita had planned to take his sister Gaynor out for a birthday celebration. Instead he got drunk alone.

Nobody felt like eating but Grace made a sandwich anyway and she and Garry sat down to watch *The Midday Show* with Ray Martin on Channel Nine. They thought it might take their mind off their problems for a while. Entertainer Karen Knowles was singing a poignant tune: "If you go away, on a summer day, then they might as well take the sun away . . ."

The words "if you go away" struck a chord with the lifelong partners. Without a word they looked at each other. Both were thinking the same thing. Tears welled in their eyes. "To us it seemed as if (the song) was almost a message that she'd gone . . . that we'd lost her," Garry said later, his voice choking with tears.

About the same time John Cobby decided to drive to Wollongong to visit close friends to see if they had been in contact with Anita. Perhaps, he hoped against hope, she was staying with them.

Chapter 11

That day, Tuesday, February 4, was hot, bloody hot. Det Sgt Graham Rosetta wiped perspiration from his forehead with the back of his hand as he turned off the main highway and drove around the side of Prospect Hill, five kilometres south-west of Blacktown. It was just past 2pm. He had never been along this road before but it was pretty out here. Like a little piece of country right in the middle of the city. There was an abandoned sandstone church on the top of the hill with a pioneer graveyard all the way down the side, to road level.

Rosetta loved the country life and hoped to return to the bush one day. He'd been raised in a small town in the NSW Riverina district and had always planned to breathe the fresh rural air again. His job had brought him to the city but living at Emu Plains, a suburb of Penrith, 20 minutes drive west of Blacktown, almost compensated for being away from the country life.

As a senior detective at the Blacktown police station, "Rosie" Rosetta was in charge of a very large section of men who handled volumes of Sydney's crime. Today a new crime would join the list. He was a professional cop. He worked hard and expected no less from his men. He was a tough man, but understanding, and his peers respected him.

It was his day off when his boss, Sgt First Class Tony Cassimatis, called him in on this urgent matter. It wasn't unusual to have a day off interrupted. He collected Sen Const Hugh Dundas from Blacktown police station on his way through. It was Dundas' day off too. The two men could not have looked less alike. Rosetta, a thickset man with a strong face, dark hair and olive skin, could have passed for an Italian builder. He looked powerful. Hugh, on the other hand, had wide flashing eyes and styled blond hair. His dashing looks usually attracted the attention of women. They were chalk and cheese, but they got on well together.

The road was narrow as they raced past the fields and homesteads, turning left into Reen Rd, about three kilometres from the highway. It was an L-shaped, badly-tarred road cutting into the green paddocks on either side. From the top of the street there is a noticeable dip in the road, like a roller coaster track. Not all of the land had been cleared and the tall, slender ghost gum trees grew so close in parts that their branches overlapped. Looking to the left, there was a row of huge metal electricity conductors, massive things a hundred or so metres high. Beyond them was dense bush which reaches down to Prospect dam, a kilometre away. Rosetta wiped his brow again. He could see a summer storm brewing in the distance.

At the top of the road were three uniformed police from his station who waved them through as he slowed down. Rosetta pulled up on the side of the road. A dry gust of hot air blasted his face as he opened the car door. Tony Cassimatis greeted them. "Young woman, aged between 18 and 30, naked, large blood loss. No ID," he reported. "Who found her?" Rosetta asked. "Farmer who lives up the road. Found her over there," he said, indicating a spot 70 metres west of the roadway. It was known as the Boiler Paddock, where once all the old cows were kept together.

Rosetta and the other two strode through the knee-length grass to where a group of police congregated. At their feet lay the body of a woman in a large pool of blood. Rosetta could tell she had been dead for some time. "Find anything?" he asked his colleagues, as he knelt beside her.

"No ID, just this ring on her finger," came the reply.

The woman was lying on her stomach, her left arm under her chest. Her head rested on her right arm and her eyes were open. There was a concentration of blood on the ground around both sides of her head. Even though she was face down you could see cuts coming up from her throat and extending into her right ear.

Back in the car, Rosie called his unit. It was going to be a long night and they were going to need all the men they could get for this one.

The media has a knack of knowing what's on and where. Channel Nine already had a news helicopter in the air on the way to another job when the station received a call. Nine's crime reporter Steve Barrett remembered, "It was the perfect day for flying, so clear. We were on our way to Campbelltown where a boxer had been killed a few days before. I received a call on the blower to go to Prospect, there was a report of a body found. When we flew closer to the area I knew this was something big. The place was swarming with cars, ambos, and cops. If you can, imagine this pocket of green country-like space with tall gum trees, cows in paddocks, horses, a line of huge power lines running down the other side of the road. And all these cops. There was definitely something on. There was about 20, 30, 40 cars there and as we hovered closer I could see the big brass were out here, inspectors and the like, and then I *knew* it was big. And there were no other journalists there.

"As we landed in the paddock I could see a group of cops huddled in a circle in the middle. I walked over and I could see them standing around the body of a woman, lying there like a crumpled doll in a large patch of blood. The cattle were standing around looking bemused. I just kept wondering where the hell were all the other journos. It was too good to be true but they all arrived about 10 minutes later."

Det Sgt Ian Kennedy was already there. He'd been in the city office of the Homicide Squad about to have lunch when someone walked in and said, "Looks like there's a job on at Blacktown." Instead of lunching, he found himself detailed to the paddock at Prospect. There he witnessed the body of a young woman who had been murdered with animal-like ferocity.

Kennedy was tall and hulking with rosy red cheeks and a winning grin. The subtle waves in his hair were worn brushed back from his forehead and his sideburns had a tinge of grey. He sometimes walked with a slight limp in the cold weather, the legacy of arthritis from his rugby days. The ailment had forced him to give the game away.

Kennedy spoke to Det Paul Davies, from Blacktown police station. He and his partner Det Sen Const Phil Gaspert had been called to the scene. Both had been summoned from home after working back on a job that had only finished at 5 o'clock that morning. They had been on duty the previous night when Const Murphy filled out a missing person report about a young woman.

"Sarge, I'm not positive, but I think this could be the nurse who was reported missing last night at the station," Davies said. They walked through the grass to where the body was lying. Because of the blood on her face and her injuries the constable still wasn't sure. The dead woman looked different. The hair looked very similar though — thick and wavy.

Davies and Gaspert jumped in the car and drove back to Blacktown police station. Davies pulled out the report and photo from Const Murphy's pidgeon file. He looked at the photo. He was sure it was the same woman. Her hair was the giveaway.

Police scientific photographer Paul Hamilton was already busy when Ian Kennedy arrived. A senior constable with the Physical Evidence Section at Penrith police station, Hamilton had attended many murders in his years with the police department. He had worked with most of the police here at some stage on other murders. A gentle man with a pleasant nature, he snapped away. Every possible angle had to be captured on film not only to aid police in their hunt for the woman's killer but as evidence for a court to view. He took notes with a silver pen. After two hours he'd just about finished. He joined the others in another search of the paddock, looking for anything that could give police a clue to solving this murder. There was nothing.

Dozens of uniformed police combed the road and the grassy areas alongside the wire fencing. Up and down the area they walked, looking under rocks, beside old tree stumps, through piles of dumped building and household waste. There were bricks, bits of timber and an old red and white striped mattress with the springs showing. They found nothing. Dozens of birds chirped, the crickets were loud and cows plodded through the paddocks. You could hear the buzz of cars and trucks in the distance on the busy Great Western Highway.

The Government Medical Officer, Dr Joe Malouf, was busy making notes. He was known as Gentleman Joe. A small, always obliging man in his mid 50s, he had attended many crime scenes over the 25 years he had been on the job and was hardened to such sights. But several officers noted this day that both Joe and his young attendant seemed upset by the nature of this murder.

A Russian wedder ring, three entwined bands of white, yellow and orange gold, was on the ring finger of the dead girl's right hand. It seemed to be the only clue to her identity. Sgt Kennedy removed the ring, put it in a small plastic bag and placed it in his coat pocket.

Rosetta went back to his car and drove 300 metres up the road to where Reen Rd turned right into a dead end. John Reen's was a colonial style house, not grand, but comfortable red brick. His family had owned the land for years and worked it with a herd of dairy cattle. They had sold sections of it to the Water Board and were now leasing it back. The road leading through the property was named after his family.

The 43-year-old farmer was a short, stocky man, with a round face and big round eyes. His hair had started to recede but you usually couldn't tell because he wore a hat most of the time. He was badly shocked by what he had seen in his own paddock. He told Rosetta that he had noticed his cows were acting strangely in the area known as the Boiler Paddock. "They had been milling around about 100 yards off the roadway in the Boiler Paddock," he said. He wasn't sure then whether it was the Sunday or the Monday when he first saw the cattle in the paddock but he said the cows grouping there was an "unusual occurrence".

He told Rosetta that around 8am that morning he had left his home to go to the Camden cattle sales and noticed the cows were still milling in the same area. He didn't check the herd but when he returned three hours later they were still there. "From the elevated position in my truck I could see there was an object in the paddock around where the cows were milled," he told police. "I went home and about half an hour later I decided to go and investigate the object. I rode down to the Boiler Paddock on my motor bike and when I got to where the cows were milled I saw a naked body lying face down on the ground, lying beneath a tree with the head facing towards the tree. I could see it had been there for a period of time and after seeing the body was female I rode back to my house and telephoned police." He told journalists later that day, "I couldn't believe it was a human lying there. I thought it was a dog."

Rosetta took notes as John Reen said that he remembered hearing loud noises either on the Saturday or Sunday night coming from the Reen Rd area. The noises had been loud enough to wake him from his sleep. "It sounded like shouting or screaming." He was used to people using the road at night, joyriding or as a lover's lane, and although the noise had continued for a short time he had taken little notice of it and went back to sleep.

On the way back to the paddock, Rosetta thought about the victim and the agony on her face. He would never forget that look of terror. The corpse was put on a steel-framed green stretcher, covered by a blue plastic tarpaulin, secured and then carried back through the paddock, over a barbed wire fence and into the back of a waiting ambulance.

Chapter 12

There was a loud knock at the Lynchs' door. Ian Kennedy had always hated this moment. It didn't matter how many times he'd done it before, it didn't make it any easier the next time around. "I'm Det Sgt Kennedy from the Homicide Squad and this is Det Const Heskett," he told Grace and Garry, motioning to the policeman, Garry Heskett, at his side.

The policemen were asked in. The Lynchs looked hopeful as the big man began to speak. Then he broke their hearts. "We have found the body of a young woman in a paddock at Prospect. There was no identification on her but she does resemble the description of your daughter."

The Lynchs drew their breath and closed their eyes. Garry looked up at the detective and said, his voice breaking, "I could wish it was someone else's daughter but I can't, can I? They would then have to go through what we're going through."

"Was she brutalised?" Garry remembers asking. Kennedy and Heskett hung their heads in affirmation.

"I have a ring here that the young woman was wearing. Can you tell me if your daughter was wearing a ring like this?" Ian Kennedy asked. Garry took it, examined it and shook his head. He had never seen it. His wife shook her head. Then "Yes, Anita had one similar to this," Kathryn said as she took the three entwined bands in her hand. "John gave her a Russian wedder, that's what they're called, but I can't be sure if this one is Anita's. It looks too aged and rusty." The rust was her sister's blood.

At that moment John Cobby, driving to Wollongong, heard a radio news report that a young woman's body had been discovered at Prospect. He feared the worst and telephoned his in-laws' home. They were too distressed to speak to him. Kennedy handled the situation, gently breaking the news. John Cobby began to cry.

At around 5.30 that afternoon Kennedy and Heskett returned to the Lynchs'. John Cobby was there, sitting on the back steps. He identified the ring taken from the body of the woman as the one he had given his wife then he broke down. He couldn't face going to the morgue to identify her.

On the way to Westmead Hospital mortuary, the officers talked to Garry Lynch and his other son-in-law, Kathryn's husband Ray Eedens. They talked about Anita and their words seemed to comfort the men. Grace Lynch had wanted to accompany her husband — "She's my daughter, too, and I would like to see her. I'm a nursing sister." Kennedy dissuaded her and said it would be better if she remembered Anita the way she was. Garry Lynch was ashen-faced as he was led into the sterile-smelling hospital. He followed Kennedy and Heskett into a room with a big glass panel covered by a curtain. The curtain slid back. "I was looking at this poor battered little face," Garry remembered. He went weak at the knees and thought they would buckle. "Then I felt this big, strong hand grab me at the back of the neck. It was Garry Heskett who had hold of me and he was like a pillar of strength, the most wonderful strength."

Garry looked again at the white sheet covering the still form lying on the table in front of him. There was just a little square not covered by that sheet. It covered everything but the woman's face and her hair. Joe Malouf had washed her face well but the bruises were clearer now. "It took me a while to fully identify her," said Garry. "She was in a bad state of damage. I was able to identify her, though, from the line of her nose that wasn't hurt. Both her eyes were very badly damaged and her mouth too. Her chin line and her hair gave me the real lead. I could see bits of grass caught in it as the ringlets were laid out behind her. I had no idea really how bad her other injuries were then. Nothing prepared me for seeing the brutalising of our lovely daughter's face. It didn't look like her but it was." Crying, he remarked later to Garry Heskett that, after what she'd endured, "I thank God that she didn't survive."

On the way back Kennedy took Garry to the Boiler Paddock. "You think I'm cruel," he said, "but in time you'll know that it was important to know where Anita died." Garry broke down, but later came to accept the wisdom of Kennedy's action.

Chapter 13

Police converged on Blacktown police station. By late afternoon a squad of about 20 had formed a task force team which assembled in the second floor Detectives Office. This room would become the base for the Anita Cobby murder investigation.

Before the police team was even briefed, journalists were preparing their reports of the grisly discovery. By nightfall that Tuesday they were gathering outside the police station. All attempts to get past the front enquiry counter had failed. A few police roundsmen with contacts at Blacktown managed to ring the Detectives Office direct. But at that stage police barely knew more than what was offered on the evening news bulletins.

Seasoned journos shook their heads in disbelief while discussing the vicious acts perpetrated on Mrs Cobby. They waited all through that night on the footpath for a scoop, for anything.

Upstairs in the station, the mood of the police was much the same. The men and women listened as they were addressed by Graham Rosetta and Ian Kennedy, joint heads of the investigation. This was the procedure of the time when the specialised team, in this case the Homicide Squad, joined forces with the local cops.

It was an unusual combination. Sergeants Rosetta and Kennedy were as different as the seasons. Rosetta, the quiet, hard-nosed local detective with a pronounced wariness of journalists, was a stark contrast to Kennedy, a jolly city cop whose job in the Homicide Squad and as a footballer brought him into frequent contact with the media.

Kennedy had been a rugby footballer of note. As captain of the famous Randwick club side known as the Galloping Greens, he was one of the code's favourite sons. In the late '70s he led his team to two premierships. He was christened "Speed", for his lack of it when he played on the wing in his early football days. The name stuck and now anyone who knows him would never think of calling him anything else. Even his bosses.

Football was one thing Speed Kennedy had in common with Graham Rosetta who had been graded with the Balmain rugby league team in 1968. His police work, however, kept him from spending much time on the field.

Kennedy brought with him from the Homicide Squad Sen Const Kevin Raue and his work partner Const Garry Heskett. Both had a sound knowledge of the local area, Raue living in Penrith and Heskett having only just joined Homicide in town after three and a half years with Blacktown detectives. Both were having a day off after working on a double Vietnamese murder at Fairfield in Sydney's south-west and a Yugoslav murder at nearby Cabramatta the previous week. Garry Heskett was at Police Headquarters following up some information about a case when Speed Kennedy was called out to the Boiler Paddock. Heskett accompanied Kennedy back to Blacktown.

Rosetta had at his beck and call a room crammed with his own detectives as well as a station full of uniformed police. Because of the brutal nature of this killing and the fear that a maniac was loose in the community, police hierarchy in town let it be known this murder investigation had their full support and the use of other specialist squads to catch the culprit or culprits would be encouraged.

During the briefing that evening the team was informed that the dead woman had been positively identified as the missing nursing sister from Blacktown, Mrs Anita Lorraine Cobby. Constable Davies' instinct proved right. "His intuition narrowed down the scope of the investigation and saved the team valuable man hours," Sgt Kennedy said later.

There was very little to go on. Anita Cobby's body was naked. There was no trace of her clothing after a search of the paddock and surrounding area. She had no known enemies, no criminal background and no-one could offer a motive or a reason for her being in a paddock far from her home. Police had no murder weapon and could only surmise that she had been killed with an axe or a small shovel. A search of the area had failed to find a thing.

Anita's movements before her death had to be established.

Two of her nursing colleagues had been to dinner with her on Sunday night. One of them had dropped her at Central station. This was known. The nurses had to be interviewed. A running sheet charting the investigation had to be started. The running sheet, a procedure used in all major investigations, is a 24-hour-a-day log of all incoming information no matter how seemingly irrelevant. It includes statements, records of interviews, details of arrests, raids and operations. It is the journal of the case. The job of keeping the Cobby investigation's running sheet fell to pregnant Const Sue Kain, whose organising skills ensured all enquiries were checked as they came in.

Police clutched at straws. Perhaps the post-mortem, due to be performed that night, might arm them with more information. The farmer who discovered the body mentioned something about hearing noises in the area a few nights before. Maybe that was something to go on.

Clues were few but the basic rule of police investigators is that the first 72 hours of an investigation, particularly a murder investigation, is crucial. So they got to it.

Chapter 14

Speed Kennedy stayed a while after dropping Garry Lynch and his son-in-law Ray home from the hospital. Garry had walked through the front door and lowered his head in grief when he saw the expectant faces of his family. Perhaps they had thought that maybe, just maybe, the girl at the morgue wasn't Anita. There was no good news. "We all just hugged each other and wept," he said.

Kennedy and Heskett sat and talked to the shattered family. Kennedy knew what they were going through as he had lost his four-year-old son when he was hit by a car. Kennedy noticed they appeared to be in control of their emotions but the experienced policeman knew they must be in deep shock. He knew they were too numb to take in everything but they remained alert while he told them what he knew of Anita's death. He believed in being honest at times like this but his gentleness ensured the grieving parents were spared the shocking details. He did tell them she had struggled violently for her life.

Kennedy knew at that stage Anita's body had been in the paddock for up to two days, that her throat had been cut, and that she had several fractures, one to each shoulder it was thought and at least two to her hand. She had a lot of bruising, some to her face, as Garry had seen.

A post-mortem would be carried out later that night, said Kennedy. That was necessary to determine the exact nature of Anita's injuries, the time and cause of death. In his own mind, however, he was sure she'd died of blood loss from her throat wounds. Kennedy vowed to the Lynchs that the killer would be caught but that police needed the family's help and support.

"The police helped us cope from the very first moment," Garry Lynch told reporters later. "They were totally honest with us from the start and told us everything." Ian Kennedy tried to prepare the family for the inevitable tenacious intrusion of the media into their lives but left it up to the Lynchs to decide whether they would speak to the press or not.

"We decided then we must see this thing through for Anita's sake," Garry said. "We wanted our daughter's killer caught as soon as possible."

Later, Garry Lynch and John Cobby gave statements to police at Blacktown police station. At that stage, everyone was a suspect. Speed Kennedy asked John Cobby: "Did you kill her?" and "Did you get someone else to kill her?" Cobby couldn't answer. He collapsed at the desk and sobbed.

Garry Lynch told reporters later, "Det Kennedy and I had a long talk about the horror of the whole thing and he said to me, 'I want you to go and love your wife and love your daughter and all your family and cherish the memory of your dead daughter and leave the rest up to us.'"

This average Sydney family could have no idea of the impact their tragedy would have on the public. As the details of the murder slowly surfaced in the media over the next 24 hours, the public's shock turned to outrage. The nation was transfixed as the Lynchs bravely told the world about their beautiful lost daughter.

The phone at the small Blacktown home rang hot with calls from stunned friends and grieving relatives. Even experienced journalists and photographers, their compassion numbed over the years by covering many such tragedies, now found themselves moved by the calm strength of this family in mourning.

In the privacy of their own home, the Lynchs were able to share their memories of Anita. Garry remembered the last day he spent with her, Friday, just two days before she died. "After breakfast we were sitting around the kitchen table. Anita was drawing. She had taken it up again as an interest. She sketched some sea shells and then she needed a fish. I went through an encyclopaedia and found a picture and asked her would that do. She put some time into the drawing and it had a marine feel to it. I looked at it and told her the detail on the shells was very good. She looked at it again and said, 'Dad, do you know we are coming into the wonderful age of Aquarius? That's 1000 years of love and peace.'"

Now they thought of all the wasted plans. The things Anita would never do. They were pleased she'd taken up her art again. John had bought her an oil painting kit for Christmas and Garry enjoyed watching her draw. He remembered the huge painting she did for her major art exam in the HSC. She had giggled when she told them she'd called it "Cows' Intestines". It was a mass of blues and greens. It was still in her old bedroom. And she had enrolled in a Spanish course and talked about the possibility of becoming an air hostess. She had told her parents her nursing would be an advantage.

Garry had thought that the upheaval in her life, her separation from John, was beginning to settle and she was accepting her new life. "She said to me that she loved John with all her heart and she would love him all her life. But she knew they wouldn't be together again."

Chapter 15

There was nothing out of the ordinary about homicide and local detectives working together on a case. Both groups had a free hand to run the investigation as they wished. What *was* unusual was for two senior officers from different departments working on the same case to report daily, in a formal manner, to their own superior officers. This was essential due to the high profile of this investigation, even after only one day in operation. It was a two points command system that worked well. Cassimatis would report to his own superiors and Homicide Squad head Det Insp Ken Webster would in turn inform the hierachy of the Police Department who then briefed the politicians right up to the Police Minister and the NSW Premier, Neville Wran. Each had requested to be informed daily of the investigation's progress.

One of the most important jobs for the senior officers reconstructing Anita Cobby's last movements was to read the crime intelligence data and monitor the public's information. Every shred of information on the running sheet had to be assessed. "In a sense we were lucky to identify Anita quickly," Kennedy said. "If she hadn't been a local or hadn't been reported missing then it could have been some time before we tracked down her identity. She had never been in trouble and never been fingerprinted. Those first hours of finding out about her were vital".

Never had there been so many hands on deck for an operation at Blacktown. Everyone was devoted to the task of solving this crime. Police from other stations, other districts and interstate, too, volunteered information they thought might give a lead to the identity of the killer. Said one officer later: "If the bosses had known how much manpower and how many hours went into this murder investigation they would have been shocked. There were heavy budget restrictions so days off were tallied up and taken later, no overtime was sought and many of the blokes worked on their days off." For those involved, every case not of an urgent nature was put on hold and leave was cancelled. Over the following weeks the operations room at Blacktown became more than just a base for the men and women working on the Cobby case, it became a home.

There was a sense of frantic urgency surrounding the case. As Speed Kennedy put it later, "There was a maniac out there, loose in the community. We didn't know what turned him on and we didn't know if or when he would strike again."

As required by NSW law, a police officer attended the post-mortem of Anita Cobby. It was conducted by Dr Joe Malouf at West-mead Hospital. Sen Const Hall and Sen Const Paul Rynne, both plain clothed detectives from Blacktown, got the job. Rynne was a heavyset man with thick, wide hands but the effect was softened by his baby face and short, neat beard. His father, Vince Rynne, was a senior officer in the same district. Having a father who was a cop and working in the western suburbs had given Paul an insight into the area. He knew the street language, the haunts of the crooks, and, most of all, he knew the locals. Nothing much surprised him any more, but now he was shocked by the ferocity of the attack on the young woman. Outwardly he was calm, but the sight of Anita's body would cause Paul Rynne shattering long-term effects.

Back at Blacktown police station, the investigation into Anita Cobby's murder was well underway. Rynne reported to Rosetta the results of the preliminary post-mortem. It confirmed their initial guesswork about the cause of her death: loss of blood due to the severe throat lacerations. She had been sexually assaulted, sustained fractures to her hands and had extensive bruising across her body.

Now hundreds of local criminals, and specifically sex offenders, were checked out. This was going to be a big job. Hours and hours of sifting through intelligence data of known offenders in the district only drew blanks.

Detectives Phil Gaspert and Paul Davies went to Sydney Hospital to see Anita's two colleagues, the girls who had last seen Anita alive. They brought the women back to Blacktown station to take statements from them. Crying, shocked and bewildered, Lyn Bradshaw and Elaine Bray recounted every last detail of their movements that Sunday: how they had finished work, had changed at the hospital and then left around 5.30pm for a Lebanese restaurant. After dinner they parted outside the restaurant around 8.45, Lyn dropping Anita off outside Central station.

The detectives were gentle in their interrogation of the women. They gradually prised information from them. Anita was reliable, of strong moral fibre, did not take drugs or drink excessively and had only casually dated two men since her marriage breakup. As far as they knew, nobody held a grudge against their friend. Anita wasn't the type to attract enemies. And that was it.

Meanwhile a small group of detectives returned to the murder scene that night to try to reconstruct what had happened. They talked about the possible course of events and the probable course of events. Did Anita catch the train to Blacktown? If so, did she sleep through her stop and have trouble getting home or did she alight at Blacktown and meet someone, catch a taxi or accept a lift? The police reached no conclusions. They had too little to go on. A further search of the Boiler Paddock uncovered nothing. They returned to the station.

Later, police had their first lead. Const Davies, on his own initiative, decided to check the station's telephone message pad. One entry caught his eye. It said residents in Newton Rd, just a short way from Blacktown railway station, had telephoned after seeing a screaming girl dragged into a car on the Sunday night. A search by uniformed police at the time produced nothing but the residents had given a vague description of the car involved. An HG or HT model Holden Kingswood, dirty white with a lot of grey primer on the back and boot lid. The investigation team needed more, but at least this was a start. It was the only thing they had to go on, so Graham Rosetta gave the lead top priority.

Well after midnight the Cobby investigators called on the McGaugheys. "It was early in the morning but the people there were very helpful. They understood the urgency," Rosetta said. Linda McGaughey, a 14-year-old schoolgirl who lived in Newton Rd with her family, had been watching television in her home at about 9.50pm when she heard a loud, fearful scream and ran outside. From the front of her house Linda saw a man sitting with his legs protruding from the open passenger door of a dirty white Holden car parked along the street. "He was dragging into the car a dark-haired woman who was screaming," Linda said. "He had hold of her by the arm and shoulder and I could see she was trying to get away. She was trying to struggle free."

Shocked, Linda called out to her older brother John, who was inside the house and had heard the screaming too. John ran towards the car but, as he got near it, the door slammed shut, and the vehicle was driven away with its lights off. He ran out onto the footpath and watched as it disappeared into the night.

Across the road, 16-year-old Paul Hodson had also heard screams. He thought it was his Maltese terriers yelping but when the cries continued he ran to his front door. "I saw a car driving past and as I ran to the driveway the car had reached the next door neighbours' driveway," he said. "I saw that it was an off-white coloured HJ Holden sedan and its lights weren't on. There were two people in the car, the driver and a passenger in the middle of the back seat, high in the seat. As I ran out, the passenger looked back at me and I saw that he was about 18 to 20 years of age and he had fair-coloured hair, short at the front and over his ears and it was sticking up on top." The car had increased speed up the road to an intersection, and, said Paul, "the passenger kept looking at me. As the car accelerated away I saw a fellow run from a house across the road and he called out, 'A girl has been picked up by two guys in that car!'"

Hodson ran back inside, quickly pulled on some shorts and set out with his next-door neighbour and his girlfriend to look for the car. The three drove around the area for about 10 minutes. When they didn't spot the car, they returned home.

Linda and John McGaughey were upset by what they had seen. They told their brother Paul about it when he arrived home with his girlfriend Lorraine Busher about 10 minutes later. When he saw how shaken his brother and sister were, Paul decided to look for the woman. He and his girlfriend asked themselves where would someone take a woman they had abducted? They drove to Reen Rd, a popular lover's lane because of its isolation and convenience, being just a five-minute drive from Blacktown and a minute or two off the main highway.

"About three quarters of the way down (Reen Rd) I saw a red Sigma Scorpion car parked on the left hand side," Paul told police, "and a bit further down the road I saw a 1970 model Holden parked on the right hand side of the road and this car had grey primer paint on it. I couldn't see anyone in the car. I went further down the road and saw a grey Ford, about a 1962 model, on the right hand side of the road." Nothing that fitted the description given by his brother and sister. Thinking they were looking for an HG or HT model Holden, not an HJ, the pair drove straight on and continued searching other spots for about two hours before giving up and going home. While Paul and Lorraine were out in the car, the McGaughey family reported the abduction of the screaming woman to Blacktown police, just in case.

Although there was no strong evidence to go on, police knew the time of the abduction fitted into the general time frame of Anita's disappearance. They would, for now, assume the screaming woman was Anita.

The investigators worked through the night, calling in several orders of takeaway food to feed the troops. No-one even noticed that they were eating hamburgers for breakfast. The senior investigators sat around exhausting theories again, about the events that had taken this woman from the train station to the Boiler Paddock. They were puzzled that her clothing and her bag was missing. They knew the bag's contents included a leather wallet, sunglasses, a hair brush, cigarettes and a novel. And they needed that murder weapon. To help search for it they planned to bring in some cadets from the Police Academy in Goulburn for an emu parade in the paddock along Reen Rd. Every blade of grass would be searched. The killer must have left something behind.

They went to the paddock again. Photographer Paul Hamilton wanted another look around. He grabbed his camera. A group of tired, unshaven detectives emerged from the police building at daybreak.

The cicadas were loud, even at that hour, heralding a scorcher. The early morning was already muggy. The police combed the paddock but, again, found nothing.

Chapter 16

At 6am, Wednesday, February 5, Grace Lynch opened the front door. On the step was a nervous young journalist from *The Sun*. He offered his condolences, apologised for the early hour and asked if he could have a few minutes of her time. Grace told "of the girl we loved very much". "My husband Garry and I have prayed earnestly for the last two nights that Anita would return home and walk right through the door," she said. "He (the killer) must have been sick in the mind — like some sort of psychopath. People like this need desperate help and some sort of treatment. Anita was just so harmless and helpless in the hands of this monster."

It struck the reporter that even in the depths of grief, this loving mother couldn't bring herself to express bitterness about the person who had taken her daughter's life.

The phone rang on. The media was camped at the door. Grace informed reporters the family was shattered when told by detectives of the extent of Anita's injuries. "We just did not know whether to believe them, it was all so devastating," she said.

Her grief was shared by Australians everywhere. That day, one of the investigating team was quoted in an afternoon newspaper: "She was butchered, only animals could have done this," he said. The newspapers reported that Anita Cobby had fought vigorously for her life and in doing so sustained bruising to her head, torso, fractures to her fingers, bruising on her arms, legs, cheeks and back and damage to her shoulders. But the most horrifying injury was the lacerations to her throat. They extended deeply from ear to ear.

The investigation gathered momentum but, as Grace Lynch said later, "The days became a nightmare of unknowing." The family did its best to adjust to the shocking reality of Anita's death. "I felt like I had this terrible sickness and I was never going to be well again," she said. Kathryn was devastated by her sister's death. She adored Anita and later said in a television interview, "It all seemed too hard to grasp, too hard to believe."

The case gripped the country. Newspaper sales and TV ratings soared as the population sought more knowledge of the young woman cruelly murdered in the prime of her life by, it seemed, a deranged monster. The public embraced the image of this woman who had served the community well by caring for the sick. Newspapers sold out as soon as they hit the news stands. A newspaper seller at Sydney's Central railway station remarked at the time, "I haven't sold papers like this since the birth of the Broderick nontuplets in the '70s. People were just hanging onto every word about those little babies. And now people want to see whoever did this dreadful thing caught."

The Anita Cobby murder was the talk of Australia. Commuters read the headlines on their way to work and discussed the details with total strangers. "Oh, what about that poor girl found in the paddock yesterday, the poor thing" . . . "Whoever did this is a maniac" . . . "They should hang the bastard when they catch him" were common sentiments.

Sydneysiders were appalled that such a crime could happen in their city. Blacktown people, well used to their locality being criticised, were ashamed it had happened in their backyard. Everywhere people were scared. A monster was lurking.

Outside the Blacktown police station a handful of journalists had been keeping a vigil, hounding the uniformed officers at the front desk for information about the investigation. The enquiry officers were frantically answering calls from the public, and now, from the media. A press conference was organised and attended by three of the detectives. They didn't have much to say but at least it placated the journalists.

The investigation team looked dog-tired. Speed Kennedy was wearing the same tie and shirt he had worn the day before. The police appealed to anyone who may have Anita's clothing or had seen a woman wearing similar clothes to come forward. Police showed one of Anita's white nursing uniforms. On the inside of the back collar was a label with black printing "SYDNEY HOSP. A. COBBY" and the letter B beside it. The uniform was flashed across TV screens that night with updates on the investigation.

The makeshift Operations Centre in the Detectives Office at Blacktown hummed with activity. Detectives were deluged with enquiries and information from the public and media. Kennedy stopped off to report to the head of the Homicide Squad, Det Insp Ken Webster, at the CIB in the Sydney Police Headquarters on his way to Blacktown every morning and still managed to be in the investigating office by 8am. The hour-long drive from the city to the western suburbs in the morning peak-hour gave him time to toss ideas around in his mind. Graham Rosetta had a similar briefing with his superior, Det Sgt Cassimatis, before his own daily conference with Kennedy and the Cobby investigation team.

Each morning and afternoon, the officers would bring themselves up to date with the running sheet and the progress of any interview or operation. "There was so much reading and research that had to be done," Det Kevin Raue said. "It was so important to keep up with what the public was telling us. We had to stay on top of everything that was passed on and follow up whatever we believed was worthwhile."

Mid-morning on Wednesday the 5th brought yet another trip to the paddock, still barred for everyone except police. This time Det Supt Ron Stephenson and Det Insp Webster were on hand to be briefed by investigators and brought up to date with the inquiry.

Dr Malouf was sought again for advice on the injuries to Anita Cobby's shoulders. He believed they had been fractured but planned to conduct an X-ray today. Police needed to construct a picture of the force used to commit this crime.

By now the Lynch family was under siege. But the media was generally gentle. Garry was the spokesman for the bereaved family. Journalists found him an emotional man whose grief welled to the surface, his kindly hazel eyes filling at the thought of what had been done to his eldest daughter. The very memory of her would make his voice falter. It was often left to Grace to pick up the conversation and finish the sentence while her husband composed himself. This softly spoken, overpoweringly calm woman was the strength of the family.

The Lynchs were struggling to come to terms with the murder

but they were prepared to grieve in public if it helped find their daughter's killer. The dignified way in which they coped with their plight was beamed into the loungerooms of millions across the country, and their fortitude awed a nation.

Work continued inside Blacktown police station. Detectives Kennedy, Rosetta, Raue and Heskett went back to the paddock with Paul Hamilton in the late afternoon to search the lower part of the ground in case anything had been missed. They drew a blank.

The inquiry was then split into three sections. One sought taxi drivers who may have seen Anita at Blacktown railway station. Cabbies were on the police's suspect list. *Everyone* was on their suspect list. The second continued to follow up hundreds of reports about known sex offenders. The third handled the flood of daily calls from the public volunteering information that might help.

This last was a massive task. In fact the information supplied by the public led to the charging of many people with unrelated drug offences, sexual assaults, thefts and housebreakings. It also provided police with new intelligence data to add to their files.

Outside the station, journalists were still waiting on the footpath for a breakthrough in the investigation. Every reporter who had formed a working friendship or contact with any one of the police in Homicide or at Blacktown, now wanted to call on that understanding. But friendship or no friendship, the police needed the help of the media and they knew they had a willing audience. The bare facts were given to journalists in a daily press conference. Because police had so little information, anything of value was withheld. At this stage, police themselves had no real idea what kind of killer they were dealing with.

Inside the Detectives Office, paperwork was attended to into the night. By now the phone calls from the public were pouring in. The team was getting its fair share of attention from clairvoyants and fortune tellers. All of these leads, no matter how tenuous or seemingly bizarre, had to be checked out. The task of handling these was given to Garry Heskett. It was a distraction from the mainline of enquiries but he handled every one of the calls with diplomacy and tolerance. He became known as the Officer In Charge of Clairvoyants. He even took one of them out to the paddock. "Every caller who thought they could offer assistance had to be given the same degree of respect," Heskett said. "One woman was convinced she could solve the crime. She was hounding us and said she needed to set the mood by being in the area where the crime had been committed. I met her there and she put her crystal ball down on the ground and after a while she started to chant and shake her crystal ball, saying she was getting vibrations, messages. She was fishing for clues from me and said the killers could be found near a kindergarten. After a few minutes I got fed-up, packed her up and went back to the office."

Later, a round table discussion was held over coffee with most of the team present in the meal room which now doubled as a conference room. At 10pm the investigators headed home for some much needed sleep, too tired to carry on that night. It was Garry Heskett's birthday. The day had come and gone without him giving it a thought. He arrived home too late to enjoy his usual family birthday dinner. His children slept soundly as he crept to bed through the darkened house.

Chapter 17

By 6.30am on Thursday, February 6, Speed Kennedy was already on the job, sitting in the North Sydney radio studio of 2UE breakfast announcer Gary O'Callaghan. Kevin Raue had already pre-recorded a re-enactment of Anita's last known movements and to that was added traffic and train noises to make the re-enactment sound authentic. He retraced her steps from Central station to Blacktown where she alighted. The re-enactment was played and Kennedy was interviewed about the progress of the investigation. O'Callaghan appealed to the public to come forward with any information they may have had.

Tony Cassimatis arrived at Blacktown station about the same time. He was a little earlier than usual but he wanted to clear up some local enquiries before the Cobby investigators arrived. It wasn't long before the morning silence was interrupted by the telephone ringing in his office. It was a member of the public, on his personal line, saying how they had heard the appeal for information on 2UE. Cassimatis took the caller's information and hung up. The phone rang again straight away. Then some of the other phones started ringing. Within a few minutes all 15 telephones in the Detectives Office were ringing. The lone man answered as many as he could. When the first police began to arrive at 8am Cassimatis was still going, exhausted. And he was furious. No-one had informed him of the phone-in. All the calls were logged and checked but the exercise turned up nothing of value. Still, it did keep the investigation in the minds of the public.

During the 8am meeting, a call came through about a suspicious car seen at Prospect dam. It had been reported by the local ranger. He said there had been hoodlum-types in it at the time. The report was checked but it bore no fruit. About the same time, the buses carrying 200 cadets left Goulburn for the two-hour trip from the country police academy to the paddock. The cadets, from Secondary Class 208, were joined by members of the Mobile Field Command, the Communications Section, the Trail Bike Squad, the Air Wing and the Rescue Squad that had scoured the area the day before. Local detectives were there again, and, of course, the media.

The police were all dressed in overalls and shorts. Anyone who didn't have a hat was given one to wear because of the extreme heat. The cicadas were deafening. At the makeshift command point, a drive-in movie theatre less than half a kilometre away, Speed Kennedy divided the searchers into teams, assigning a detective with a portable radio to lead each one. The searchers were shown one of Anita's uniforms and told what clothing she had last been seen in. Kennedy directed the teams to stand about an arm's length apart and walk in a single line across the field so as not to miss a centimetre of ground.

Some had to climb up mounds in the ground while others crawled across logs, over and under fences, all the while maintaining a single line. It was a thorough search of the whole area but at the end there was disappointment. Nothing that could assist the investigation was found. All that was turned up was an old blue shopping bag, a dirty blue T-shirt and pieces of rubbish. At 3pm the group gathered at the drive-in again for debriefing.

The day-long operation was something for the media to run with that night along with a major announcement from Parliament House. It had been just two days since the body of Anita Cobby was found and now Neville Wran, Premier of NSW, offered a $50,000 reward for information which would lead to police securing a conviction against the nurse's killer. The amount was soon doubled.

The detectives, weary from their day in the relentless sun, returned to Blacktown to sift through the day's paperwork and return calls from people keen to help. All mental patients with a history of violence and sexual crimes had to be checked. Two detectives were assigned to make up a list of suspect names, research them and check alibis. Every detective was out following leads but again by the end of the day not one hopeful sign had emerged.

At midnight Rosie, Speed and Raue sat around a table sipping cold beers and trading theories. By now they'd gone over every shred of information and yet they weren't even sure the woman the McGaugheys saw dragged into a car was Anita Cobby. "The worst part was the delay in finding out what happened to her after she left the train," Kennedy later said. "We didn't know whether she caught a cab or walked. But we were quite satisfied she caught a cab because of what her parents and girlfriends said about her being loath to walk late at night. She would either ring her father to come and pick her up or catch a taxi. And just the night before she disappeared she promised her estranged husband on the phone she would ring her father to collect her from the station if she caught the train home."

The police traced and retraced Anita's last movements. According to Lyn Bradshaw, she had been dropped at Central station around 8.45pm. If this was so they surmised she probably would have missed the train to Blacktown which left about that time. If she had caught the next one it would have arrived at Blacktown at 10.05pm, too late for the McGaugheys' sighting at about 9.50pm. "That's why we were convinced she caught a taxi from the station and the McGaugheys' sighting was another woman. It seemed obvious that she had been abducted and our first concern was that her taxi driver was the killer," Kennedy said.

Chapter 18

Friday, February 7, shaped up to be a busy day for the police with a full schedule of checking suspects and following up information. Much time was spent answering the calls from the public and media. "The media fired everyone up and anything suspicious was reported in record time to police," said one investigator.

John Laws, the popular radio talk-back host, created a furore on his morning program on 2GB. He had secured a copy of a telex sent from the Government Medical Officer's office to Police Headquarters. It was addressed to Assistant Commissioner Ross Nixon. The report detailed explicitly the lines of investigation, facts about the victim and her family and the findings of the GMO, Dr Malouf. At that time, all of this information was highly sensitive. The full extent of Anita Cobby's injuries had not yet been revealed publicly.

Laws told his audience he found the report to be very distressing and had considered its contents for many long hours. He found the details of Anita's injuries so horrific he couldn't bring himself to talk to anyone about them, including his wife. But, after hours of soul-searching, he said, he believed he had a duty to make the report public "if only for people to be aware of what torture and degradation this poor woman went through."

He read the report. It told how Anita Cobby's head was almost severed from her body by the knife wounds to her neck. The slashing at her throat had severed the aesophagus, carotid artery, and her trachea. The lacerations were so severe that the GMO had been unable to take semen samples from her mouth. She had extensive bruising over her body, severe lacerations to her hands. Within minutes the station's switchboard was jammed. The calls continued all day and spilled over to other radio stations. The public was horrified. Police stations everywhere were swamped with calls from outraged listeners. The Blacktown police station switchboard jammed. Police Commissioner John Avery was angry the information had been leaked. There was concern it would hamper the investigation. An Internal Affairs inquiry was launched immediately to flush out the leak. The police on the case were questioned but cleared later that day. They settled back down to the business of solving the crime. The person who leaked the report has never been identified.

During the enquiries, a train guard told police he was sure he had seen a woman matching Anita Cobby's description alighting from the Blacktown train at 10.05pm on the night she had gone missing. If this passenger was Anita, the person the McGaugheys had seen was not. The taxi theory strengthened but still a lookout was kept for suspicious-looking vehicles that fitted the vague description of the car the McGaugheys reported. Local hotel car parks were checked, as were known spots for dumped vehicles.

Police appealed for the woman who was pulled into the car on Sunday night to come forward, but there was no response.

The background reading and research continued to be an onerous task for the team. That night the wrap-up conference took place well past midnight over cups of strong coffee in the Detective's Office. On many of the detectives' desks, pinned by a paperclip to the government-issue calendars, was a photo of Anita smiling beneath her mop of hair. It was as if she was reminding them to keep going. The theorising continued. Anita, the caring nursing sister who'd never been in trouble, would not voluntarily have been anywhere near the paddock in Reen Rd that night. Making love in cars definitely was not her style, so she *had* to have been there against her will. Someone must have forced her to go there.

The reasoning continued on the way home. Raue's house at Penrith was on the way to Rosetta's. They talked all the way during the 20-minute trip. "We never reached a conclusion in those discussions, we just theorised and tried to rationalise the situation we were faced with," Raue said.

The weekend with fewer interruptions than during the week was an ideal time to catch up on the vast backlog of reading and research in the office. But time was also found to visit, once more, Newton Rd and Sullivan Rd where the Lynchs lived, and ideas were tossed around again. The local hotels were checked in the hope of spotting the car seen by the McGaugheys, Saturday being a good time to do so because more people would be patronising the pubs. The tour included the Prospect Hotel, the Doonside pub, Lalor Park Hotel and the Sportsman Hotel at Blacktown.

Several suspects were questioned and alibis investigated, but all leads drew a blank. In the evening the hotel circuit was completed again and then, for the frustrated investigators, it was back to the office for the usual discussion over a cold beer before a midnight departure.

Someone had the idea of re-staging Anita's last hours in a desperate bid to jog memories. Sunday, February 9, was chosen for the re-enactment. It was a long shot but police had so little to go on. Blacktown uniformed constable Debbie Wallace was chosen to play Anita Cobby, tracing her last known movements from the time she was dropped off at Central railway station. Police by now were growing convinced that Anita had set out on foot for home after alighting from the train and that she *was* the woman the McGaugheys had seen being abducted. "Constable Wallace was the ideal choice because of her similar height and appearance to Anita Cobby and we hoped the re-enactment would prompt anyone who had seen Anita on that train or afterwards to tell us about it," Graham Rosetta said.

Debbie Wallace was also a good worker, fitting in straight away with the investigative team. The detectives were glad to have her help. She wore similar clothes to Anita and boarded the 9.12pm train from Central Station's Platform 8. Police walked the length of the train with her, interviewing every passenger on the journey. It was exactly one week after Anita's fateful trip. They showed passengers a colour photograph of Anita. The whole procedure was filmed by the media. At one stage, it was noticed Const Heskett was missing from the group. And so were the journalists. After a quick search he was discovered at the rear of the train conducting a media interview about what the police were looking for and how the public could help. A colleague remarked later, "This was a classic example of why he was nicknamed 'Hollywood'. There was no harm done. It was just a funny incident and everyone took it as some light relief during a serious job."

After alighting from the train at Blacktown, Constable Wallace stopped to talk to the media. Outside the station, she told them the most difficult part of the exercise was taking one of Anita's nursing friends out shopping to buy clothing similar to that which Anita had been wearing that night. (As it happened, the clothes were not a good match. Grace Lynch later said that Anita would never have worn such tight-fitting clothes as she never liked to show off her figure.) Then Debbie Wallace set out on the brisk 25-minute walk to the Lynchs' Sullivan St home. Detectives tailed her as she set off from the brightly-lit shopping centre into the darkness of the residential area. A westerly was blowing and it was an oppressively hot night as she turned the corner into Newton Rd, where the McGaugheys had reported the abduction, just a few blocks from the railway and the police station. Twice cars pulled up in the darkness alongside the attractive woman. Did she want a lift? asked the occupants. Both times police hearts pounded as they patiently watched and secretly hoped for the break they'd been waiting for. Debbie Wallace turned the occupants of the cars down and they drove off. Both cars were checked out. Nothing.

The police didn't disturb the Lynchs that Sunday night even though the re-enactment ended right at their door. Instead they went back to the station and sat down to coffee and hamburgers and another session of talking the case through. Speed Kennedy later recalled, "At that stage we were despairing. There were no clues, no suspects. It seemed like we were walking into a dead-end."

One of the things that kept puzzling the police team was why Anita had walked home from the station. Her family had said she was always careful. Her usual practice was to call her father to pick her up, or she would catch a cab. "We couldn't work out why she would walk instead of catching a cab," Kevin Raue said. "Normally there are lots of cabs at the railway station and it was a good half-hour walk to her house from there."

Later Garry Lynch tried to fathom his daughter's decision to walk. "I have taken that same route 20 times trying to fathom why she walked home that night. I was told at that time the telephones at the station had been vandalised and were not working so if there were no taxis there and she couldn't call Anita wouldn't have had much choice. It was a hot night and, knowing Anita, she would have felt comfortable about walking home. She was an active girl and she would have enjoyed the walk on a nice night."

Chapter 19

At the 8am conference on Monday, February 10, it was decided a number of the investigating team should be at Pine Grove crematorium and lawn cemetery for Anita's funeral later in the day. It is common for police to attend the funeral of a murder victim as a mark of respect but also, in some instances, to mingle with mourners who may be suspects for the crime.

At the funeral, nurses, colleagues of Anita, wept as they formed a guard of honour for the flower-draped coffin. Lyn Bradshaw carried a single red rose. The Lynchs bore up well and the media, although they filmed the event, kept a distance from the immediate family.

Grace and Garry Lynch walked into the chapel, arms linked with their daughter Kathryn and her husband Ray. Grace wore a delicate piece of black lace across her shoulders and carried a Bible in one hand. Inside the chapel, the white-uniformed nurses stood on either side of the aisles, holding hands throughout the service. The minister, Reverend Sweeting, had married Kathryn and Ray the previous year. He read the 23rd Psalm, "The Lord is my shepherd . . ." and he spoke about Anita's death. "The horrific circumstances of her death have ingrained in our minds that there is something terribly wrong with human society," he said. "We feel hostility that this should have happened to such a beautiful girl . . . it's a shame that in the past months she had begun to branch out in life to discover her own particular creativity. Paints and brushes had been bought and the lessons commenced. Art had been in her family for generations and it was her passionate drive to express the beauty and value of life — that drive for personal and individual survival was seen in her courage in death."

John Cobby wept. He was too distraught to recognise friends

and had to be supported by his family after collapsing. Garry Lynch remembers that day as "the saddest, most depressing day of my life". The family retreated to Garry's niece's home in Katoomba.

As the mourners left the cemetery, sharing their memories of Anita, the investigators returned to Blacktown to find her killer. They fell back into the routine of checking the running sheet, interviewing suspects, checking alibis.

By now other matters, put on hold when the Cobby case took precedence, needed attention. Rosetta, a workaholic, had a tremendous workload, but he somehow managed to handle all his cases. Tony Cassimatis, too, in ill-health before the Cobby investigation, had his workload doubled. Raue and Heskett were now called away from the investigation to speak urgently with one of the men they had recently charged over a Yugoslav murder at Cabramatta they had been working on the week before the Cobby murder. He wanted to give them vital information about that case. It was a necessary interruption. No information that would assist in the solving of any crime could be ignored. That done, they returned to Blacktown for a 10pm finish with a meeting in the office. On the way home Rosie and Raue, as usual, traded theories.

That night Speed Kennedy was pulled over for speeding down the freeway on his way home.

Chapter 20

Tuesday, February 11, started out just like all the other days, with a morning conference and a check of the running sheet. But today was different. It was the day of the first real breakthrough in the hunt for Anita Cobby's killers. It came when Graham Rosetta followed up a telephone call from a man who said he had some information. He told Rosetta he was acting for a group of four people who could help the police investigation. The group wouldn't meet police and he was to be the go-between, their spokesman. A meeting was organised. The man told Rosetta that a fellow named John Travers and some associates, including Mick Murdoch and Les Murphy, had stolen a car just days before the murder, the number plate unknown. The car was thought to be green but had been resprayed grey after the theft. Someone had actually seen the men in the vehicle on the night of the murder. The informant also told Rosetta that the car's special mag wheels had been replaced. It was thought the car had been dumped. Several members of the public had already informed police that Travers was a man capable of a brutal assault.

After a meeting with the man, Rosetta was confident his information was worth taking seriously. "We started to piece together a bit of a pattern with John Travers and his associates," Rosetta said. "From information the public had already volunteered, we knew Travers was a person known to carry a knife and that he had violent tendencies. He was wanted for questioning over a sexual assault the month before."

Ian Kennedy recalled, "With the information about the grey car and knowing about Travers' background, we started to think there might at last be light at the end of the tunnel."

Now police concentrated their efforts on looking for Travers and the other men. Travers wasn't living at home at the time but was just drifting from place to place. This new development was of such importance that it wasn't leaked to the media for fear of losing this line of investigation. Even today, police still refuse to discuss the information relating to the informants for fear of revealing their identities. But 18 months after the murder, the man who acted as a go-between for the group said in a newspaper article that only one of the four informants ever spoke face to face with police. He said he agreed to help the investigators track down the men by "dressing rough" and driving through the far western suburbs checking on houses where the killers were believed to be hiding. It was crucial that none of the suspects knew Travers was under suspicion.

At the following morning's conference, two things attracted the police's attention. On the running sheet, the Mount Druitt police station reported two drifters in a car. They might be worth checking out. The same station also reported a sighting of a grey car in Shalvey, a Mount Druitt suburb, that might be the one the McGaugheys had seen. Both pieces of information were checked out. The drifters were just that and had watertight alibis and the grey car had disappeared.

At 3pm Kennedy and Rosetta called a meeting of the police on the case. If Rosetta's informant was right about Travers and company, they were looking for locals. Where would a local go? A team would check out the Doonside Hotel, reportedly one of Travers' haunts. Others were to do the usual hotel rounds and look for the resprayed car. Still nothing was found.

Rosetta liaised with his informant again. They needed more information on Travers, who his associates were, where they all lived, what they did and where they went during the day. The police were working under extreme difficulties. Great care was taken to treat the information confidentially because the informants feared for their lives.

That night Graham Rosetta and Kevin Raue went back to Reen Rd. They knew the area was a popular lover's lane but what struck them on this and previous visits there was that people were still using it despite its close proximity to where Anita was killed. They quizzed the people parking there and with discretion they even checked out some of the alibis offered when they asked the occupants of cars what they had been doing on the night of February 2.

During one of these checks on Reen Rd, other officers came upon a worker from their own station in a compromising situation in a parked car. The startled colleague was respectable, middle-aged, and with someone definitely not their spouse. "The person was very embarrassed about the situation and we were taken by surprise but still they had to be checked out. Nothing was ever said after that. The matter was left there," the officer said.

It was a 6am start the next day for the detectives to execute a search warrant for a house at Lalor Park after a telephone tip-off that drugs and a suspicious car were on the premises. The car fitted the description the McGaugheys had given. The search of the house proved fruitless but maybe they had something with the car. The McGaugheys were brought to the station to identify the car but they could not. The day seemed to have been a waste.

Groups of media still maintained a vigil on the footpath outside the station. They could not afford to miss even a second of the investigation. This day the three television crime reporters, Steve Barrett from Channel 9, Sean Flannery from 10 and Norm Lipson from 7, decided to take a half-hour break and walk through the Blacktown Mall, around the corner. They left their crews behind. The rivalry was always intense between the stations so the three had made a pact. They agreed to cover for each other if one missed something. "But if one uncovered something on his own that the others didn't have, that was different. You kept it to yourself," remembered Lipson. "The deal was if something happened while we were away, the crews went ahead to cover it and we'd catch up later. We wandered back across the street with icecreams in our hands to find our crews gone. We ran into the station but there was no-one there who could tell us what had happened. Our first thought was that an arrest was on and we'd missed it. We all panicked. Then my crew came down the road and told me two lots of TRG police had come screaming out of the station and they'd lost them in the rush. We all jumped into my car and then Flannery's crew turned up. They'd followed a decoy car. That meant the Channel 9 crew were on their own. Flannery and I grabbed Barrett by the tie and made him call them on the portable radio to find out where they were. He didn't try very hard but we heard his cameraman say, 'Don't worry, Steve, we're here. There's a raid on and we're the only ones. We've got it all.'

Flannery and I thought our goose was cooked. We demanded Barrett find out where they were, so we could go there. His crew reported they had shots of the police busting down a door. Luckily for us the raid was unsuccessful. There was no-one home."

At 8.30pm the police once more made the rounds of the local hotel car parks to check on vehicles. This still seemed to be their best lead. It was an earlier finish than usual at 11pm.

At the 8am meeting on Friday, February 14, discussion centred around the scientific difficulty of establishing Anita Cobby's blood group. It was vital for the forensic scientists to know this so samples taken from her body could be tested to give clues to the killer's identity. The body wouldn't provide a definite blood grouping, perhaps because of the length of time it had been out in the paddock in the summer heat. Sydney Hospital couldn't locate the grouping either. It wasn't on Anita's employment files and the Lynchs weren't sure themselves.

During the investigation there had been a request from South Australian police authorities for tissue, blood, hair, semen and other samples from Anita Cobby to be preserved. The police scientist told the Cobby team of a new form of genetic finger printing being used in England that could positively identify suspects to murders. The process would be available in Australia in the near future so the preservation of samples would be required if police wanted to use the method. Unfortunately that request came too late. Anita Cobby had already been cremated and all samples taken during the post-mortem had already been used. The process is called DNA and it was first used in NSW in the Janine Balding murder investigation and trials in 1989 and 1990.

Inspector Pat Toohey, Ken Webster's second in command in the Homicide Squad, was visiting from the CIB that day to look at the operation's progress. It was a busy day checking suspects' alibis and following up information from the public. Most of the afternoon was devoted to reading information that had accumulated on the running sheet. Saturday and Sunday too were spent checking suspects and catching up on information from the sheets.

On Monday, February 17, Rosetta and Raue parked nearby the Travers family home at 5 Tich Place, Doonside, to observe the premises even though they knew Travers was on the move. A few blocks away, in Criterion Crescent, they interviewed a man who had called the station reporting hearing a man in the paddock next to his home crying in the early hours of the morning after the night Anita disappeared. He said the man sounded in despair, really anguished, and he heard the words, "It's a murder, it's a murder, oh no, it's a murder." It fitted the time frame of events. Perhaps the man was the murderer. Perhaps it was John Travers. It was only a short distance to his home. The police searched the paddock hoping to find a weapon or anything that may give them a clue. They found nothing. But the two policemen discussed the incident while they did the usual rounds of the local hotel car parks before turning it in around 8pm.

The next day, Kevin Raue met Paul and Linda McGaughey and Stephen Hodson at Police Headquarters in the city and took them to the 21st floor office of police hypnotist Sgt Roger Johnson. Desperate to glean more information about the car the abducted woman was dragged into, police suggested the three be hypnotised. In separate sessions, Johnson told them to close their eyes and imagine they were on a beach, sitting on a beach chair, enjoying the sun and feeling it beat down on their skin. Sgt Johnson played a cassette of beach sounds, waves crashing, gulls squawking. He told them each had a balloon on a string tied to their wrist. A light breeze was blowing. The arms with the balloon rose slightly, as if the wind had caught it. He told them to switch on a video in their mind of what had happened in the street that night and rewind it, telling him what they saw, frame by frame. Kevin Raue, observing, claimed the session was so real that he worked up a sweat just sitting out on the beach with the three. Their story of the screaming woman being dragged into the car was confirmed, but they could give no new leads on the make or number plate.

Chapter 21

It was hard to sustain the pace of the inquiry in the absence of any new leads. Wednesday, February 19, was shaping up as just another day to read the running sheet and check and double-check all the information from the public, just in case. A man who had committed suicide in the Blacktown area had left a note. It read, "I or my father . . . aren't responsible for the Anita Cobby murder."

Later that morning a group of Homicide officers from the city arrived at Blacktown to be taken to the murder site and then briefed in preparation for a raid on several houses in the area, believed to be haunts of Travers and his associates. The operation was fruitless.

Public fear and anger had by now reached such an extreme level that the reward for information leading to the capture of Anita Cobby's killer had been doubled to $100,000. "This is just one of the foulest crimes of the century," Premier Wran said, "and the animals responsible must be brought to justice . . . it's an unusual step to take and perhaps it sets a precedent but the foul and vicious nature and unbelievable ferocity of that girl's death warrants that those responsible will be brought to justice quickly."

One of Premier Wran's personal staff members observed in private that when the Premier was shown the autopsy report on Anita Cobby, he had been so horrified by the details that he was unable to complete reading it.

The announcement helped keep the investigation in the media and prompted more calls from the public into the Blacktown Detectives Office. That night police worked late checking out many of those calls, but nothing further was discovered.

When police arrived back at the station they spotted the journalists waiting outside on the footpath. Out of the police car stepped detectives escorting a man with a coat pulled up over his head. The police, in a half walk-half jog, went straight past the journalists. The reporters fell over themselves to retrieve camera equipment and notepads. Cameras clicked, bulbs flashed and the group surged towards the front door of the station, following detectives and their "captive". Then the man with the coat dropped it and turned around. It was Graham Rosetta, sporting a wide grin on his face. One of his colleagues yelled out, "Just keeping you on your toes, fellas," and they disappeared inside.

Police met at 6am on Friday, February 21, to confirm the procedure for the operation planned to snare Travers, Murdoch, Les Murphy and five others whom they believed may have been associated with the theft of the grey-sprayed car. "We had the idea that Anita Cobby had been subjected to some sort of pack rape but we hadn't offered that suggestion publicly at that stage," Speed Kennedy said later, "so the idea of a few of Travers' associates being involved fitted the picture." Each team of detectives had Tactical Response Group officers assigned to it and around 6.45am they called again on the haunts of the eight people they wanted for questioning.

At one address in Toongabbie, a sledge hammer, popularly known among police as "the key to the door", was used to force entry. There was "slight damage to the door" according to a police report. The door, in fact, was slammed right off its hinges. A woman in the house told police the man they wanted to speak to wasn't there right now but she would have him call them when he arrived home later that afternoon. The police apologised about the unhinged door and promised to contact the Housing Commission to have it repaired. They were true to their word. Later that afternoon the wanted man turned up at the station and was cleared. "He was very good about the whole thing considering what had happened to his door," one officer said.

Rosetta, with Constables Rynne and Davies and a TRG group, finally located Travers and Murdoch at 27 Jewelsford Road, Wentworthville, a neighbouring suburb of Blacktown. This was where Travers' uncle and his girlfriend, the two who had driven Travers back to South Australia, resided. The girlfriend and her two children lived in a flat at the back of the premises. The TRG used the "key to the door" at the front while Rosetta, Rynne and Davies covered the side of the house. There was a wooden gate blocking their entry at the side. One of them kicked it, bringing the fence down as it gave way. At the same time there was an almighty crash of glass from the front of the house. As the front door gave way under the weight of the sledgehammer it clipped a huge tropical fish tank near the doorway. The door crashed through the tank, sending a torrent of water across the room, out the door, down the front stairs and across the lawn with fish flipping everywhere as it went.

Inside, Travers and Murdoch were found in bed together. The pair admitted to the car theft to Graham Rosetta, but they denied involvement in the Cobby murder. A search of the house located a sheath knife under a mattress in the bedroom the men had been in. There were blood stains on the blade. Travers told police the knife was his.

Meanwhile Speed Kennedy, Phil Gaspert, Hugh Dundas and Sen Const Shepard from Mount Druitt detectives had gone with the TRG to the Travers family home in Tich Place, Doonside, just kilometres away, expecting to find Travers and Murdoch there. Instead they found Les Murphy and his car, a white Holden station wagon, complete with gleaming mag wheels. He later admitted these had been taken from the stolen car. The station wagon, with fluffy red hearts hanging from the mirror, was driven back to the police station for fingerprinting and forensic testing. Police found nothing incriminating except a pair of sheepskin car seat covers which, according to Murphy's record of interview, belonged to the stolen car. Interviewed by Heskett and Raue, Murphy denied involvement in Anita Cobby's murder but was charged with the theft of the car.

Rosetta interviewed John Travers back at the station. While they talked, Travers sat mindlessly pricking his thumb with a pin. He would jab the pin in, pull the skin up, lick the drop of blood and do it all again. Rosetta was struck by Travers' "eerie" eyes. "I haven't seen too many sets like that," he said. "Those eyes were completely lacking emotion." Rosetta showed Travers the blood stains on the knife's blade and said, "I've examined the knife and there appears to be blood stains on it."

Travers then said, "I didn't slit that slut's throat."

Rosetta said, "I haven't suggested you did. Can you tell me if that is blood on the knife?"

"Yes, it is, but it's not her blood, it's sheep's blood."

"How do you know that?"

"Because I killed a sheep in the yard at home."

"Why did you do that?"

"Well, you've gotta eat."

"When did you do that?"

"About a month or two ago."

"How did you kill the sheep?"

"I cut its throat."

Later, Travers agreed to give a sample of his blood for testing by Dr Malouf. Travers was also charged with stealing the car but was kept in custody because police wanted to speak with him about a number of sexual assaults in the area.

Police took Murdoch on a run-around, a reconstruction of events surrounding a crime. He pointed out the site of the car theft on January 28, in front of a Seven Hills home. This was verified by the owner. Murdoch gave police a record of interview, was charged with car theft and bailed. He continued to deny any involvement in the Cobby murder. Les Murphy was bailed.

Police posted a tail on the released Murdoch and Les Murphy. They were now working hard on the theory that the stolen car from Seven Hills *was* the vehicle the McGaugheys had seen and it was Anita who had been abducted in Newton Rd. This being so, she must have caught the 8.45pm train from Central and Lyn Bradshaw must have dropped her off earlier than she thought. They had no hard evidence yet. They didn't even have the car. But if Rosetta's informants were right, then everything was falling into place.

The stolen car was a crucial piece of evidence, police were desperate to find it. The vehicle was vital because it could yield clues about the murder — fingerprints, blood perhaps. The recovery of the car became their prime focus over the next two days.

Police had information from the running sheet about a burnt-out car found by a council inspector in Doonside. The inspector had photographed it and stuck an order on it that said if it wasn't claimed within seven days it would be removed by the council. The car fitted the make and the model of the one they were looking for. Kennedy and Raue drove to Powers Rd to look for the vehicle, but couldn't find it. The area was partially thick bushland, although there were many trails through it, used by the locals to dump rubbish and the kids to ride their bikes. *Polair*, the police helicopter, was brought in to search for the car, without any luck.

That evening police went to the Paterson house in Tivoli Place, Doonside, to see if the couple knew the whereabouts of Gary Murphy, Les' brother. They wanted to talk to him about his association with Murdoch and Travers. The police already had information showing the Patersons to be associates of Gary Murphy. Judith Paterson answered the door. She told them she didn't know where Gary Murphy was.

Ray Paterson was taken back to the station for questioning. On the way Speed Kennedy told him Travers and Murdoch were believed to have stolen a car from Seven Hills a few weeks before and brought it to his home. Paterson denied any knowledge of the car but when told there was information the car had been used in the Cobby murder, Paterson replied, "Shit, I don't know nothing about that" then admitted the stolen, resprayed car *had* been collected later by Gary Murphy who told him later that he had dumped it and burnt it. The admission was a significant gain for the police.

After giving a statement, Paterson agreed to show Kennedy where he thought the car had been dumped, but repeated he knew nothing about the murder of the nurse. He said he had seen the TV news reports but did not know that the burnt car was the one police were looking for. They searched the bushland around Powers Rd, Blacktown, for 90 minutes without success. Armed with the information Paterson had given, Raue and Heskett went to Debbie Way at Toongabbie, to Dulcie Murphy's house. The mother of the Murphy brothers said she hadn't seen the vehicle police were looking for and couldn't help them with the whereabouts of her son Gary.

That night most of the research back in the office centred on the criminal data held on Gary Murphy. Now the midnight discussion came alive.

The Saturday morning conference concentrated on the recovery of the stolen vehicle. The investigative team was briefed at regular intervals during the day by the surveillance police on the comings and goings at 5 Tich Place. Sharon Travers said she didn't know where any of the men were. Police again went to Powers Rd, to look for the stolen car. No luck. Dulcie Murphy was visited again by detectives looking for Gary. She told them she hadn't seen him since he went out in his EH Holden earlier in the day.

By mid-afternoon everyone was catching up on reading the running sheet and sorting out the information it contained. At 5pm Const Bates, the station control officer, spoke to Kevin Raue about a request from John Travers who was still being held in custody. The prisoner had asked for his aunt, the girlfriend of his mother's brother, to be contacted. He wanted to tell her he was alright and ask her to bring him some cigarettes.

Kevin Raue called the woman. "I identified myself and told her Travers was at Blacktown on a car stealing charge and he'd asked if she could bring him cigarettes," Raue said. "I chose my words carefully, not knowing who she was."

"Oh, I'm glad you called," the aunt said and burst into tears on the phone. "I need to talk to you about John. I was going to come and see you in any case but I was a bit scared." They agreed to meet at 6pm at Wentworthville Leagues Club. She'd be wearing a light blue dress. As Raue hung up the phone, it struck him that this may be the break the team so desperately needed.

Chapter 22

At 6pm Kevin Raue, dressed in brown pants and a casual beige cotton jacket, waited on the front steps of the Wentworthville Leagues Club. It was a busy place and from where he stood he could see every car that entered the large car park. He eyed each one from habit, looking for that grey Holden. But now he was also looking for a woman in a light blue dress. Rosetta and Heskett waited for him inside, sipping beers in the main bar.

Raue shifted nervously and waited. He had been looking at a young woman for about five minutes and she had been watching him too. Finally, he approached her. "I called her by her christian name." "Yes, that's me," she replied. He offered her his hand and smiled. She was shaking and kept looking around to see if anyone was watching her.

"I wasn't sure if that was you or not," she said, stumbling. She was embarrassed to meet a policeman. "My arms were showing and I was conscious of the (needle) scars over them," she recalled. She had been a drug addict. "But he was really kind to me and he didn't worry about the marks."

From what this woman had said on the telephone that afternoon, Raue knew she was going to talk about John Travers and Anita Cobby. "She was very nervous and shaking so I walked her around the back of the club and we sat in the front of the police car to talk. I asked her if she thought he had murdered Mrs Cobby and she said she thought he was capable of it because he'd raped before."

She considered the circumstances of the murder and the way Travers had behaved in the past, his attitudes to women, the way he hunted them. She told him she was close to Travers, he trusted her and confided in her, especially over the last six months. He considered her his aunt even though she wasn't married to his uncle. They did have a child together, however, and planned to marry in the future. She also knew Mick Murdoch and the lifestyle of the two.

Travers, she told Raue, had been involved in a vicious homosexual rape and another rape of a girl last year, both interstate. In each he had used a knife in a similar manner to the killer of Anita Cobby. Travers' details of the homosexual rape had particularly scared her. She had thought many times after hearing his account of the assault that he needed some sort of help. She really felt he was capable of committing a murder like this and knew that he still carried a knife.

"I knew what John was capable of — not many others did," she said later. "I just gave the detective a rundown of what John was like and then sent him away." When they finished speaking, she got out of the car, ran past the club and disappeared into the night.

Raue, a man whose blunt, matter-of-fact demeanour masks an acutely perceptive and caring nature, walked back into the club feeling that this woman was telling the truth. "It was encouraging to have somebody so close to Travers onside and although there was no evidence at this stage I was feeling good about the information. I told the other two of my confidence. She had come across as very sincere and seemed genuine about wanting to help."

Back at Blacktown police station the other investigators were briefed on Raue's meeting with Travers' aunt. Then Rosie and Raue headed for the Sportsman Hotel to check the carpark for the stolen car and to have an ale before heading home.

Over their beers they decided to ask the aunt to come to the station the following morning to take the cigarettes in to Travers. Maybe he would incriminate himself to her.

That night, for the first time in three days, a handful of scruffy policemen were driven home. They hadn't shaved, they were worn-out and they were tired of living on take-away food and snatching a few hours sleep here and there at the station. "Garry came home wearing the same underpants he left in on the Tuesday morning," said Suzanne Heskett. "He was dead on his feet. He had called me from work and said he wanted a baked dinner. He was home a few hours and then it was back to the office."

At 8.30am the next day Kevin Raue called the aunt and asked

her to come in to see John Travers. Normally visitors and prisoners' requests aren't allowed but these circumstances were special and police were hoping the breaks were finally going to favour them.

About 10am the woman arrived at Blacktown police station. She recalled: "I went to the Detectives Room upstairs and Det Raue spoke to me and said he felt John knew something about the car and that if he told me anything would I please relay that to the police. I thought that was alright. I thought it was possible he had stolen a car. I had seen him do it before. He would steal one, and leave it out the front of the house, open, for any of his mates who'd want to use it. If the little rotter had taken a car, I thought, he may well tell me."

All police on duty that day were briefed about the next move. The station controller was told to tell Travers that his message had been delivered. "Travers' aunt wasn't given any questions or told what to say," Raue said. "What she would say to him was left entirely up to her."

The woman was taken from the Detectives Office to the ground floor cell block where Travers was being held. Raue waited behind the front counter of the station where he could see her down the corridor, through a wooden door with glass panelling.

The woman spoke to Travers through a small square grille, at eye level in the middle of the solid steel door. She gained the impression that the cell was set down lower, that you had to go down a step to get into it. She could see Travers' cell had a small wash basin, a toilet and a bed. There was an adjoining exercise yard.

"He was just standing there in his jeans because that's what he was wearing when he was taken from the house. He'd been asleep with his jeans on, I suppose," she later said. "He was not hurt at all when I saw him, I expected a mess. He was being fed really well and he was even making jokes about the policemen giving him cups of tea and calling him 'China' and offering 'how about a couple more sugars?' and telling how they gave him extra sugar and biscuits and stuff like that."

During the 25-minute conversation between the pair, Raue watched as Travers' aunt nervously shifted from one foot to the other. Several times during the conversation he saw the woman take the prisoner's hands in hers through the small opening in the door.

She would press his palms to her face, stroking them gently while she listened.

Then he said it. Travers told his aunt he had killed Anita Cobby. She felt numb, like she wasn't really there. She burst into tears. "I had my hand on his face. I just said, 'Oh, no.'" Through the turmoil she kept talking to Travers. She kept her shock under control until she left his sight.

As she walked down the corridor away from him, the pictures of the paddock, the face of the smiling nurse that she had seen on TV and the newspaper descriptions of how this girl had been slaughtered came flooding back to her. "I thought, 'Well, John, you've got to be punished, you've got to be stopped. If I don't say something you are just going to walk away. Next time it might be worse.'"

As she came down the corridor, Kevin Raue saw her face and knew their plan had worked, that Travers had confessed to the killing. Without a word, he escorted her out of the station office and into a small adjoining courtyard where she began to cry. He caught her as she collapsed into his arms. "It's him," she sobbed. "He told me the whole story. It's him and Mick Murdoch, Gary, Les and Michael Murphy. He was big-noting himself. He said, 'We all talked about it but I was the only one with the guts to do it.'"

The woman cried and shook uncontrollably. Even though she had half suspected Travers of killing Anita Cobby, it had been a dreadful shock to her to hear him admit it so openly. She was escorted upstairs to the Detectives Room again and Raue took her into a glass office in the corner of the room where he gave her a cup of strong coffee to settle her nerves.

Raue told Rosetta of Travers' confession. Rosie said nothing. He just looked at Raue. Then slowly a smile crept across his face. He was elated. He lit a cigarette. This was the turning point.

Travers' aunt composed herself and told the detectives everything Travers had told her. "They asked me if I was prepared to assist them any longer," she remembered, "and I said, 'Yeah, of course.'" Raue said later, "It was quite obvious to me she was very distraught about giving Travers up but she was more concerned about what had happened to Anita Cobby."

A statement was taken straight away, outlining Travers' confession. Speed Kennedy was contacted at home. He'd planned a late start so he could spend a few hours with his wife and sick son. Kennedy's son Matthew had been born the previous November with serious bowel complications. The baby had been in hospital until the middle of December. He had difficulty feeding and two days before the Cobby investigation started, Speed and his wife found out their child was profoundly deaf. Of the untimely extended periods away from home because of the investigation, Kennedy later said, "It was tough on my wife and it was hurting me. I couldn't see the little bloke as much as I wanted to."

Now, over the phone, Rosetta, Kennedy and Raue agreed to take advantage of the situation that had presented itself. They would wire up Travers' aunt with a tape recorder to secretly record his confession. It would be the strongest possible evidence against him they could have — a confession in the killer's own words. There are strict rules about the use of listening devices. The only way it could be done was to have a judge provide a Supreme Court warrant giving the police authority to use a hidden recording device.

Raue went back to the glass office and discussed the plan with the woman. By now he had a good rapport with her, she trusted him. Rosetta was in and out of the office, puffing on cigarettes while listening to the details of Travers and the woman's conversation as they were being typed. She also told them Travers had asked her to help him escape from the country with his girlfriend.

Travers' aunt was told she could have no contact with anyone for a few hours. They left her sitting in a little glass office with cups of coffee and cigarettes while they planned their next move. She could see them huddled around a desk on the other side of the office. She didn't know all their names but their faces became familiar as the day wore on.

Sitting there in the fishbowl office, the woman remembered the awful moment when Travers had told her he killed Anita Cobby. "My instant reaction when he told me was, 'Oh, my God. I can't believe this,' but later I could believe it — I knew." She remembered telling Kevin Raue the night before about a time she had quizzed Travers about the murder. Travers had arrived at her place with a couple of mates and a few young girls. They were all drinking and a TV news flash came on about the Anita Cobby murder. She had watched it and then looked over at Travers and said, 'You did that, didn't you John?' He had laughed. None of the others had picked up on it. He had just laughed.

She now believed that for some reason Travers wanted her to know of his guilt. She was glad in a way he had chosen her. "John told me he would take the rap for everyone and go down in history." The thought of his boasting made her sick.

Alone with her thoughts in that fishbowl she remembered another time when she had made her own children sit in front of the TV and watch news reports of the murder. She had lectured them about the dangers of wandering around the streets without telling her. They were good kids but she needed them to understand. "The Stranger Danger program was being taught in schools at that time and I wanted to reinforce that in their minds," she said. "I was scared that there was someone evil in our area doing horrid things. I was hoping as much as everyone else that they would catch the person who did this terrible thing."

Speed Kennedy arrived at Blacktown police station that afternoon. From home he'd been on the phone organising details for the granting of the Supreme Court warrant.

The police wondered how Travers' uncle would react to his girlfriend's involvement. After all, Travers was his nephew. She believed he would stand by her.

Her nine-year-old son, from her first marriage, and the couple's son, then five, were being cared for by a friend. Police collected the boyfriend at work, picking up the children on the way, and brought them back to the station. The boyfriend was worried. He knew something was up that concerned his girlfriend but police would tell him nothing. "After all, I had just disappeared that morning and no-one had heard from me," the woman said later. "I hadn't been allowed to phone anyone to tell them I was alright."

Police explained the situation to Travers' uncle who agreed to help in any way he could. Said the aunt, "He was great. He had to deal with me. By that time I was a real mess."

The children whiled away the afternoon in the station, unaware of what was going on. "They spent the time playing on typewriters and computers and ate heaps. The police were looking after them really well. Kept them entertained the whole time," the woman said. "That was good for them really. I had always told them they could trust a policeman and to go to one if they were in trouble, so this just reinforced that."

During their conversation in the cells Travers had asked his aunt to go to Tich Place, to his home, and give Les Murphy a message: "Get rid of the car properly because the police know all about it." He also asked her to dispose of the clothes he had worn and his knife. The police said she should go ahead and deliver the message. Murphy may lead them to the car.

Despite not knowing Les Murphy, Travers' aunt went to the house with her boyfriend. "I'd seen him once from a distance of about 10 metres, something like that. I knew Lisa, John's sister, was living with a bloke called Les but I had never met him and I didn't know the Murphys. I'm glad I didn't."

At the Travers' house the woman introduced herself and told Les she had a message from John. Murphy told her to come out to the back of the house to speak. He then agreed to go with them in the car. Travers' uncle drove, she sat in the front, and Murphy and his girlfriend Lisa Travers sat in the back. Murphy gave directions to Plumpton Rd, Blacktown where he believed the car to be. Police already had information that a car, fitting the description of the one they believed was used to abduct Anita Cobby, had been dumped and burnt several days before. Now the car wasn't there. The pair later told police Murphy seemed genuinely surprised. The woman asked him where his two brothers Gary and Michael were. They might know where the car was. He said he didn't know but he would call his sister to see if she knew where they were. He told her that the police had already tried to pin the Cobby murder on him. They stopped at a public phone box. "The connection must have been bad because sitting in the car I could hear him yelling into the phone, repeating things. His sister didn't know where the others were, he said.'

Travers' aunt remembered they were "trying to convince him, trying to get it out of Les — like we knew what he had done — but trying to find the car and getting him to admit it (the murder) to us — he was really frightened, he was so frightened." They drove around for four or five kilometres looking for the car but when they couldn't find it they returned Murphy to Travers' place.

Eventually they reported back to police. Speed Kennedy had

been busy contacting the Police Department's legal advisor, who was off duty, to discuss the legality of the recording device. He'd also called Sgt Third Class Roger Kilburn of the technical surveillance unit of the Bureau of Criminal Intelligence, at home, to put him on standby in case he was needed to wire up the woman.

The plan was then discussed with Travers' aunt. Would she consent to being fitted with a small tape recorder and try to coax a confession from Travers in the cells? She agreed. "You see, a person could only be held at the station for a certain amount of time before they had to be let go if they weren't charged with anything," she remembered the police telling her. "I kept thinking, 'they can't let him go after what he has just told me' and I thought about the sheer joy and delight on his face when he told me about the murder. I had to help the police."

There was another long wait in the fishbowl office. She didn't like being in there. She felt as if she was on show, the centre of attention. All around her everyone was busy. Leading the biggest group were Graham Rosetta and Ian Kennedy, both on the phone, checking information. There were other little pockets of activity all over the room. Oh God, how she hated being there. Thoughts raced in her head. How could John have done such a thing? John was somebody she had loved. She still loved him. But she could never condone his evil.

She recalled yet another time when she had been watching television with her sons. She remembered it was around the time the *Challenger* space shuttle blew up, killing its occupants. Mick Murdoch and John Travers had walked in during the news. They sat together at the kitchen table. "Mick was white as a ghost and he wouldn't talk. I was worried about him because he was so white. I suggested he go to see a doctor because he looked sick and he wasn't acting right. John told me I had rocks in my head, there was nothing wrong with him. John then got down with the kids on the floor and was playing and wrestling with them. He had a special touch with kids and was able to communicate with little people. Maybe that came from being around so many of his younger brothers at home." Murdoch wouldn't look at the TV. She thought maybe he'd eaten something that had made him a little off-colour. "There was no life in him, no smile in him. I know now that look meant he was disgusted by what they had done."

Police lawyer Insp Gordon Lever from the Legal Advisory Section obtained a telephone warrant from Justice Slattery of the NSW Supreme Court giving the go-ahead for the recording of Travers and any others suspected of being involved in the murder, under the Listening Devices Act. The approval was valid for only 24 hours.

Travers' aunt was carefully fitted with a small reel-to-reel recorder inside a metal box. Sgt Kilburn taped the device to her stomach. Microphones were taped to her chest. The recorder could not be seen under her clothing. He checked several times to make sure that the recorder was working. Kilburn knew they would only get one chance at this. "It was a cumbersome jolly thing, most uncomfortable," she said later. "It had little ears coming up towards my shoulders. I was wearing jeans and a fairly large sloppy joe so it was covered up. But I was petrified. I couldn't stop shaking — my voice kept cracking."

She was taken down the steps from the Detectives Office and escorted by the station controller, Const Bates, to the cell door. Raue and Kilburn waited anxiously. They were concerned that the noise of the trains from the tracks behind the station would drown out the conversation. "And we had no way of checking whether it would or not because we weren't able to monitor the conversation," Raue said.

"What blew me out," Travers' aunt said, "was that John didn't think it was strange that I was coming to see him again, because when I'd seen him in the morning I said to him I'd try to come back but usually you're only allowed one visit a day. He had said, 'Well, no worries, but if you do come bring some biscuits and smokes.'

"I went up really close so he couldn't see me properly. If he had looked he would have seen my feet stomping up and down, being so terrified, so nervous, but all he saw were my head and shoulders." She told him she had done everything he wanted — found the car, got rid of it, found and destroyed his jeans, the shoes he wore, his shirt. I told him I had done all of this. The police already had his shoes and they told me not to touch anything else."

She still needed a clue from Travers on the whereabouts of the murder weapon. "What do you think happened to that knife?" she asked Travers, moving up close to the cell door . . . Do you think that Les might have pissed it off? Did you take it with the clothes and all the other stuff of the nurse's? Did you take it to the dump?"

"No . . . It's me best knife."

"Was it?"

"I want to keep it if you can find it."

"Keep it? Don't get rid of it? Well, you're lucky I didn't find it 'cause I would have got rid of it."

Travers' aunt said later: "I wanted details from him about the murder: what they did, in what order they had raped her . . . He didn't hesitate in the slightest." On the tape she can be heard asking Travers: "Did . . . did . . . I don't know how to put it . . . did you have sex with her? Did you have sex with her?"

"Yeah."

"Did you? Did anybody else?"

"All of 'em."

At that point Miss X remembered, "John's face lit up, his eyes . . . they were inhuman. It was disgusting. The sheer joy. He was like somebody I didn't know. It was all I could do to stay. I wanted to be sick. It was horrific and it was something I couldn't cope with. He was not human and this was somebody I cared about. He was very proud of cutting her throat. He had well and truly dominated a woman. And he told me he had made her beg for her life."

After 30 minutes she emerged from the corridor. This time she was taken straight upstairs without a word and into the fishbowl office where Kilburn turned off the device. Travers, she told police, had once more discussed the murder. Kilburn checked again. The tape worked. They had him.

Another statement was taken from the woman. Again her thoughts raced. She remembered seeing newspaper pictures of Anita's parents, how she had felt sorry and had despaired for them. "What if it had been my child?" she thought. "How would I have coped with that?" Her answer? "I would want that murderer caught and I would kill him myself."

Chapter 23

That night, Sunday, February 23, the entire investigation team and Travers' aunt met near the Granville railway station. It was their base to plan the next move. The woman had told them Les Murphy was to meet a friend in the car park of the Granville RSL. A surveillance team was already set up there. She would wait behind. Now, six car-loads of armed police staked out the club. They planned to arrest Murphy as he left his rendezvous. Before the group split, Speed Kennedy addressed the team, reminding them to put aside their personal feelings about the case. "We have all been under enormous pressure during this investigation because of the media attention," he said. He asked that the wanted men be brought in without incident. The police dispersed and Rosetta, Raue and Paul Rynne hid in the back of a panel van with shotguns. They all waited. Murphy didn't turn up.

Sgts Chris O'Toole and Tony "Muddy" Waters then led their team to Granville after receiving information that Les Murphy was in a house there. He wasn't.

Detectives met again at Granville railway station. It was nearly 11.30pm now. Again Sgt Kilburn loaded the tape recorder and the plan was for Travers' aunt to go to Murdoch's mother's home in Booth St, Mays Hill, a tiny suburb near Westmead. The surveillance team had kept tabs on Mick Murdoch. They knew he was there. Travers' aunt was to try to get information from Murdoch on tape. The police would be waiting nearby.

There, Murdoch and the woman talked on the front lawn in the dark. "He didn't say much," she said later, "But he indicated he would 'piss off to Western Australia' if things heated up." After 20 minutes she left and rejoined the police team. The tape was again checked by Sgt Kilburn. The group, Speed Kennedy, Rosetta and

Rynne and the TRG squad, liaised with observation police, then moved in on the Murdoch home. It was 12.03am.

Kennedy knocked on the door and Mrs Murdoch opened it. Kennedy saw Murdoch in the loungeroom, sitting with some others. He said to him, "Michael, will you come here please?" Murdoch rose and walked to the front door. Kennedy said, "Michael, since I spoke to you last Friday about the nurse Anita Cobby I have received some information that you, Travers and the three Murphy brothers were the persons responsible for the murder. In fact the car I spoke to you about was the car you used to pick her up that night. You are under arrest and I am going to take you to Blacktown police station and talk to you further but I want you now to understand that you need not answer any questions or say anything unless you wish but anything you do say will be recorded and may later be given in evidence. Do you understand that?" Murdoch did.

Rose Murdoch said, "What's going on?" Kennedy replied, "I am from the Homicide Squad, CIB. We are going to take Michael to the police station and talk to him about the Cobby murder."

"Michael," she gasped, "What have you done?"

Murdoch turned to the police, "Let's get out of here." He was handcuffed and taken away. On the way to the police station Murdoch allegedly told Kennedy he hadn't raped Anita and that Travers had cut her throat.

Minutes later the phone rang at Travers' aunt's house. She had only just arrived home, 16 hours after leaving the previous morning. It was just past midnight. She answered the phone. Straight away she recognised the voice although the woman didn't identify herself. "What have you done?" Rose Murdoch demanded. "How dare you tape my boy and involve him with the police!" She was furious. "She told me she would get me any way she could and if she didn't, one of her sons would. I put down the telephone and thought, 'Oh, my God, what *have* I done?' I panicked, I was really frightened," Travers' aunt said later.

From that moment a Tactical Response Group guard was placed around her Wentworthville home. The police realised the woman would need protection. She was a police witness now. Placing her on the Witness Protection Program was a way of ensuring she survived to attend court to give evidence. Accordingly, her identity had to be kept a strict secret between select police and, later, those involved in the court cases. A suppression order would prevent personal details about her, her features, her name, her family's names, from ever being published. Her relationship to Travers, though, would be known. At the Coroners Court months later, magistrate Derrick Hand decreed she would be known as "Miss X".

In the meantime, Raue's team returned to Blacktown police station, picked up a search warrant and went to 5 Tich Place, Doonside, the Travers' home. A squad of 12 searched the house and yard. In a wardrobe in one of the bedrooms, Paul Davies found the jeans Travers told his aunt he was wearing on the night of the murder, the jeans with the slits in the hips. They also found some hunting knives in the kitchen drawer and a charred silver bracelet when sifting through a pile of ashes on a cement slab in the backyard. It was never confirmed if the bracelet belonged to Anita Cobby.

At 12.40am on Monday, February 24, Kennedy began to interview Murdoch, while Phil Gaspert typed. Three hours later the statement was complete.

By now, Les Murphy was also under arrest. Chris O'Toole, Tony Waters, Heskett and Davies had finally found Murphy on their fourth visit to the home of Wilma Markham in Railway Street, Granville. She later said in court that police had visited her four times between 10pm and 3am. Shortly before the last time she answered a knock at the door to find Les Murphy on her doorstep. He asked if he could stay at her place while he telephoned his solicitor about some stolen wheels. She agreed. She knew the Murphys through one of her sons who was going out with Gayle Murphy, Les' sister. The couple had a son. Then the police arrived. They found the diminutive Murphy hiding between two women under a blanket on a mattress in one of the bedrooms. At 4.15am Kevin Raue interviewed Les Murphy. Const Heskett typed. By 8.30am they had finished.

It was around 4.30am when Graham Rosetta and Paul Rynne went down to the station cells where John Travers was asleep on a mattress. Rosetta shook his shoulder, "Are you awake?" he asked. "Yeah, what's up?" Travers replied. Rosetta told him he had received further information implicating him in Anita Cobby's murder and he was going to take him to the Detectives Office to ask some questions. "Who gave us up? Les?" the prisoner blurted. As he got to his feet, Travers said, "I knew I was fucked the other day. What about the others? Have you got them too?"

Rosetta asked, "Who else are you talking about?"

"The Murphys, Les, Gary and Mick and Mick, Mick Murdoch," came the reply.

"Were they involved in it?"

"Yes," said Travers.

"Who killed her?"

"I did."

Rosetta took Travers upstairs and questioned him in the fishbowl office. While Rosetta asked the questions, Paul Rynne recorded Travers' answers on a typewriter.

By sunrise the team had Travers in custody with a taped admission and a verbal confession to the killing. They also had verbal confessions from Murdoch and Les Murphy who were also in custody. The pleasing aspect of the records of interview, police said, was that all three independently supplied the same list of names of the people involved. There was no mistake.

Speed Kennedy wanted to tell the Lynch family about the arrests before they heard it from the media. Pat Toohey, second in charge of Homicide at the CIB, was at Blacktown. He drove Kennedy to the Lynchs' home. It was early. They weren't up and had to be raised from bed. Garry Lynch remembered, "Pat Toohey said to me, 'See this man here,' pointing to Kennedy, 'he has had no sleep.' Ian Kennedy lifted his bleary eyes and said, 'We've got three but there's still two more.' I was shocked. I thought how . . . how could *five men* do this to one woman?"

Back at the station, Travers, Murdoch and Murphy gave blood, pubic hair and head hair samples to police doctor Moynham for scientific testing.

Chapter 24

Word of the arrests spread quickly. Dozens of journalists waited with photographers on the footpath outside the police station. They were joined by scores of onlookers. It was overcast and a little breezy but mothers with babies paced the footpath, elderly women chatted, men stood around with their hands in their pockets and teenagers craned their necks for a better view — all ordinary folk. One middle-aged woman stopped to ask what the fuss was about and decided to stay once she knew police had made an arrest in the Anita Cobby murder case. It was 8.30am when the first of the three men was driven on a run-around — visiting the scene of a crime. The men were taken separately to the scene of the abduction in Newton Rd, and then to Reen Rd, where all were photographed indicating to police what had happened on the night of the murder. The scientific photographer on duty that morning was Const McGraw.

The crowd had steadily grown throughout the morning to several hundred people. Six uniformed police quietly watched them from the footpath. One was Const Debbie Wallace. She helped keep the driveway clear which led down the ramp to the undercover police carpark. Each time a police car reversed out of the driveway with one of the men inside, the crowd surged forward, yelling and banging on the car. As Les Murphy was driven out, one woman screamed, "Show your face!" His head was covered with his shirt. Another yelled, "Give 'em to us women, we'll deal with 'em!" It continued. "Kill the bastard!" screamed someone else. The crowd began chanting each time one of the men was driven out, "Hang the bastards . . . hang them!" After the last car left for its run-around, a senior uniform officer stood on a small brick wall outside the station and appealed for people to disperse. They ignored him but did quieten down, for a short while at least.

Returning from the run-arounds, it was almost impossible for the cars to make it back into the police station. By 11.15am when the last car returned, hundreds of people stood across the roadway blocking the footpaths on either side. They crammed into every small space along the road. They even climbed on top of buildings and hung out of adjoining office windows to catch a glimpse of the men charged with killing Anita Cobby. Construction workers dropped a rope noose from the top of the shopping centre, across the road from the station and adjoining court.

In the middle of it all was Channel 7 reporter Norm Lipson and his camera crew. He recalled, "It was a frightening scene. The crowd was screaming for blood and when the car with Les Murphy came back from the run-around they all surged forward, pushing me and the crew hard up against the vehicle. For some reason the back window was half down and Kevin Raue put his hand up to protect himself as he tried to wind the window up. Murphy had his coat over his head and was crouched down. Someone spat right through the open window. Someone else tried to get his hands inside. My crew were filming it all. Then I saw this decent-looking woman screaming abuse. She was so loud. She went to reach inside the car, still yelling. Then my sound assistant called out, 'Hey Mum! What are *you* doing here?' We were all shocked. It had reached every one of us. As citizens we were all touched by this crime."

The men were charged, fingerprinted and taken to Blacktown Local Court through the station's adjoining doors for safety reasons. By now the crowd had swelled to around a thousand people, all calling for justice of one kind or another.

Just before noon, the three handcuffed men appeared in court. They were separated from the small public gallery by a wall of 10 plain-clothes police. Stipendiary magistrate Ross McDermid warned the gallery that no outbursts would be tolerated.

Leslie Joseph Murphy, 22, maintenance worker of Doonside, John Raymond Travers, 18, unemployed and his address given as Jewelsford Rd, Wentworthville (his uncle and aunt's home), and Michael James Murdoch, 18, unemployed, of Booth St, Mays Hill, were charged with the murder of Anita Lorraine Cobby at Prospect on February 2. While the charges were read, Travers, now wearing a blue-checked flannelette shirt, blue jeans and running shoes, remained impassive. Two unrelated charges of assault and committing an act of indecency on a woman at Toongabbie on January 8 were also read. There was no flicker of emotion on his face. He kept staring straight ahead.

Murdoch faced an additional charge of stealing a car on January 28 at Seven Hills. It was the still-missing car used to abduct Anita Cobby. All police had was a photograph, taken by the council ranger. Murdoch's eyes were fixed on the floor, as the charges were read.

Murphy was still wearing the checked flannelette shirt and jeans he had been arrested in and was barefoot. He too looked at the floor as the charges against him were read. He was further charged with receiving four wheels and two seat covers valued at $1000, knowing them to be stolen. These were from the vehicle used to abduct Anita.

Public solicitor Craig Patrick represented the three men and asked the magistrate for an adjournment. "There is no application for bail," he said. No details of the crime were given to the court. When McDermid asked Police Prosecutor Sgt Bruce Newling if the defendants had any prior convictions, he was handed a small bundle of papers. None of the prisoners spoke during the five minute hearing. The investigators, unshaven and unchanged from the day before, sat quietly as bail was refused for all men. Those charged were remanded in custody and were to appear again before the Westmead Coroners Court on Thursday, three days later. Travers also had to appear in Blacktown Court again the following week in relation to other assault charges.

Outside, the mob was growing rowdy. Citizens howled for the return of capital punishment. Newly-appointed NSW Minister for Natural Resources and the local member of Parliament John Aquilina said the Government had indicated its concern about Anita Cobby's murder by doubling the reward money to $100,000 for information leading to the arrest and conviction of the nurse's killers. The Premier, too, tried to keep emotions in check. Neville Wran said, "Everyone can understand why people are disgusted and angry about the case, but the public interest would be best served by remaining calm."

Speed Kennedy later remarked to a newspaper journalist,

"Most of these people (the crowd outside) had no personal involvement. Here they were yelling and screaming . . . I might expect people to do that for the Beatles. But with the Beatles it was adulation. This was hatred."

After the court adjourned, police again asked the crowd to disperse. But the people stayed. Just after 1pm a convoy of police cars waited in the station's driveway. Two police vehicles led the way for a small police van carrying the charged men. As they wove their way up the driveway the crowd pushed through the solid line of police who acted as a barricade. Blacktown resident Joe Gardner yelled out, "Hang them and save the country some money. Even animals wouldn't kill like that. I'd vote for the return of capital punishment today!"

Later that day, Det Chris O'Toole was still in court, this time for the appearance of Ray Paterson, charged with being an accessory after the murder of Mrs Cobby. It was alleged the 34-year-old had harboured the Murphy brothers at his home in Doonside after the murder was committed.

It had been more than 30 hours since the investigators had slept. But back they went to the Blacktown Detectives' Office. The momentum had to be maintained. Michael and Gary Murphy were still out there somewhere and had to be caught.

A telex was sent to Police Headquarters in Sydney, officially informing senior police of the arrests and supplying all the details. Then all the detectives sat down to a debriefing, tracing the course of the operation. The strengths and the weaknesses of the investigation were raised. It was also made clear that this was no time for self-congratulation. The job wasn't over until the two Murphy brothers were apprehended. Recalled one policeman, "This was important because there could have been a tendency to go home and think ours was a job well done, but Rosetta and Kennedy revved us up for the task ahead — the capture of the other two men."

That day the police were allowed the luxury of a 60-minute lunch break. Then it was back to work. A tip came in that a suspicious-looking green Cortina, 1974 model, had been sighted at Riverstone. The Murphys had been reported using a Cortina before and Rosetta, Raue and others raced to the location. They missed the men by minutes. They returned to the office at 3pm and after another debriefing by Speed Kennedy, the descriptions of Michael and Gary Murphy were circulated Australia-wide, listing them as wanted for questioning. Then it was decided there was little they could do, so they should go home and catch up on their sleep, but all were placed on standby in case the Murphys were located.

Outside, the media was still camped on the footpath. TV reporters Barrett, Sean Flannery and Lipson knew the investigators had gone home for a rest, but they still needed to be at the station in case something happened. It would have to be covered for their evening news. The trio went for a short walk. "We decided to get a haircut and ran into a former policeman, Terry Griffiths," Flannery said. "He'd been seriously injured while on duty outside the Hilton Hotel during the bomb blast there in 1978. With his compensation he'd bought a hairdressing salon in Blacktown, called Flames. He'd told us to call around. When we arrived, there was a problem. There were only two chairs vacant and three of us. Our rivalry was so intense that, of course, we didn't trust the one not in the chair not to race off and get a scoop on his own so we made Terry lock the door while Lipson and I sat down first, so Barrett wouldn't bolt on us in an emergency. During the haircut we kept looking in the mirror every time Barrett moved near the door. The customers couldn't get in but more importantly Barrett couldn't get out. Barrett insisted on the same deal when it was his turn."

Chapter 25

The next morning, Tuesday, February 25, the newspapers were full of descriptions of the fugitive Murphy brothers. Police warned the public not to approach either of them. "Michael Murphy is extremely dangerous and is believed to be armed," one newspaper read. "He is 162cms tall, brown hair and eyes, medium build and complexion and is believed to have shaved off his moustache since the last police photo was taken. He has the word "LOVE" tattooed on the fingers of one hand and "HATE" and a dagger and a heart on the other. Gary Murphy is 178cms tall, same build and complexion, but has the words "DAD" on the left forearm and "MUM" on the right. He also has a heart on his upper left arm."

The police returned to work at 8am to be greeted by jangling telephones, from the media and the public volunteering information about the wanted men. There had been many sightings of the pair on the run. They had been reported in a car and on foot in Blacktown, Seven Hills and Glenfield. One call came from a taxi driver claiming they had held him up. This was a false alarm. Some of the calls came from friends and relatives of the Murphys who claimed they now feared for the men's lives. Every call was investigated.

Pressure was intense. The nation seemed to be watching Blacktown police station and waiting for the police to apprehend these men. This time there was hope their task would be a little easier. At least now they had a positive ID on the suspects. Photos of Michael and Gary Murphy were circulated. Every major newspaper and TV station published and screened them. A squad of 12 TRG police was placed on standby in the Blacktown Detectives Office.

Garry Lynch appealed to the two men to give themselves up to police for their own safety. Through *The Daily Mirror* he said, "Please give yourselves up before anyone else is hurt." He said the men must realise how desperate their situation was. "I only hope they give themselves up before they are hurt or do something tragic. Whether they are guilty or not these men should go to the police for their own safety."

Back at Blacktown police station there was a tip-off that the Murphys were in a house in Lena St, Merrylands. Police raided it. Nothing. The detectives carried out another raid on Dulcie Murphy's house. Gary Murphy's car was in the driveway but he wasn't there. She didn't know where he was.

The station phones were ringing off the wall. Gary Murphy had allegedly been sighted in Maryong, near Blacktown. He was seen entering a house in Daraya Rd. Police asked neighbours who lived there. Yes, they were told, Murphys resided in the house. Police went over the back fence, pistols drawn. A group of TRG burst through the front door. They saw a man in the garden. He just looked up and laughed when he saw the armed invaders. "Not again!" he chuckled. Although sharing the same surname as the fugitives, he was not related and didn't know the wanted men. His family had become used to being suspects. Said one of the police, "Mr Murphy was very good about the whole thing and realised the necessity for our search."

During a half-hour break for coffee and hamburgers at 8.30pm, Granville police called the investigators to say an informant who knew another Murphy brother, Bernie, believed he might be harbouring the two brothers at his house. A search of the home turned up nothing. Police also checked with another Murphy brother, Danny, and then at Radmore Ave, Hebersham, where Gary Murphy's pregnant girlfriend lived. She told police she had had a telephone call from Murphy but didn't know where he was. Police had information she was going to meet Murphy and help him escape with a car. It was alleged later in court that police had told the girlfriend that Gary Murphy would be shot on sight. This was denied by police. They returned to the station for a 5am finish.

It was all hands back on deck by 1pm the next day for a psyching up session. Top priority was to catch the men on the run. The pace couldn't be slackened in any way. They knew they were getting closer. A total suppression of details to the media and the public was ordered. This had to be a water-tight operation. There was no room for mistakes.

Lisa Travers was interviewed and asked if she knew the whereabouts of the two Murphy brothers. She told friends she did not appreciate being tailed by the police. They were watching every move she made, hoping she would lead them to the wanted men. They even followed her to the railway station and the shops. She was adamant her boyfriend Les Murphy wasn't involved in the slaying. "He just wouldn't do it, not that sort of thing," she told one friend.

Police returned to Gary Murphy's girlfriend's home. She said she hadn't heard from her boyfriend and he had not telephoned her as planned last night.

Two late phone calls came that day. Mila Coleman, a neighbour of Dulcie Murphy at Doonside, was being interviewed by *Daily Mirror* reporter Craig McPherson when her phone rang. It was about 8pm. The caller said, "It's Mick, Dulcie's son." He wanted to know where his family was and he indicated he was in the area. "We are not very friendly with them and I was shocked that he would ring here," Mila Coleman said. After McPherson discussed the call with his office, the *Mirror* called Blacktown police with the information. The police concentrated their efforts in the Doonside area.

Then, not long after, their attention was diverted. Sgt Pringle at Macquarie Fields police station took a telephone call from a man who said he believed the Murphys were in a townhouse in Tari Way, Glenfield, a suburb of Campbelltown, a satellite city on the south-western outskirts of Sydney. The investigators rang the informant back to confirm the location. He had seen one of the brothers in the yard of the townhouse and later noticed someone peeping through the curtains of the same address.

Rosetta swiftly organised a surveillance team to rush to the area and then make contact with the informant again. Rosie and Kennedy then sat down with their team and quickly but precisely planned their next move. Sgt O'Toole would remain behind to co-ordinate the operation from the station's operations room. When the surveillance team called back they were hiding near a 1974 Cortina parked on the roadside a few streets away from the townhouse. It was the one the Murphys had reportedly used the day before and which had been under surveillance for 24 hours.

The surveillance team, equipped with a portable radio, positioned itself in a small access road near Tari Way. Police watched from inside a nearby townhouse to try to see if the Murphys were inside 22 Tari Way. If so, they had them cornered.

At Blacktown station, Kennedy and Rosetta and their team were given bulletproof vests and perspex shields. They raced to the scene in a fleet of both marked and unmarked cars. Hard on their heels was the media, some in large outside broadcast vans which flew around corners at dangerous speeds, upsetting expensive equipment inside.

The surveillance team radioed that a woman had left No.22. As night fell, TRG police had discreetly formed a ring all the way around the two-storey complex, about 50 metres back from the dwellings. It would have been impossible for anyone to leave undetected. Command post radioed back to the surveillance team not to approach the woman but to wait until she reached the perimeter of the stakeout and then bundle her into a car and bring her to Raue and Heskett. The woman, Mavis Saunders, when halted, told police Gary Murphy and his brother Michael had been at the townhouse the previous day but were not there now.

Raue and Heskett didn't believe her. They reported her statement to Rosetta over the portable radio. They would observe the house for a little longer and then take the woman back to the forward command post at the front of the units.

Minutes later Rosetta decided to raid the townhouse. More than 30 armed police circled the complex in the darkness and waited. At 10pm they would make their move. Two assault teams were set to work. The first, led by Kennedy, Rosie and Raue with five others, would enter through the front door of the house while the second would come through the back a few moments after. Rule No.1 about raids is that no two teams enter premises simultaneously because of the risk of shooting each other as they pile in.

The first signal to move up to the house was the sound of the motor of the police helicopter *Polair*, while the switching on of its spotlight was the sign to storm inside. *Polair* was ready. It hovered overhead. The first team crept up to the front yard, through the overgrown garden, and up the stairs to the front door while the second team crawled through the back yard. A TRG officer was the hammerman, the man to wield the sledgehammer. He positioned himself in front of the others.

Right on 10pm *Polair's* "nightsun" spotlight turned night into broad daylight, illuminating the whole area. The sledgehammer did its work and as the door gave way, the first team rushed through. Gary Murphy ran for his life out the back door. According to police, he made it nearly all the way to the back fence but was crashed to the ground in a sweeping tackle by TRG officer Const Donaldson. Murphy tumbled face first into the fence.

Meanwhile, back inside the house, Michael Murphy, police say, was found sitting in the loungeroom with a woman, Debra McAskill, and a small child. They were watching television. Murphy himself claims he was standing near a water heater after watching his brother dash out the back door.

Unaware that Gary Murphy had already been apprehended, police continued to search for him upstairs until some minutes later other officers came in through the back door and informed Kennedy that their quarry was in custody.

Dogs were brought in to search the place and Michael Murphy was handcuffed. The woman was taken away for questioning. Gary Murphy bore scratches on the side of his face after the arrest. His bloodied features were captured by press photographers gathered outside the home. He told police he was glad it was all over and that he had wanted to give himself up. In his fright he had urinated in his jeans. He was led away with a large wet patch on his crotch.

Mick Murphy told police on the way back to the station, "Okay, I'll tell you everything. It's better to tell you the truth than to have them believe what's been on TV. Police said he then gave a frank version of the crime.

Chapter 26

The Murphy brothers were taken to Blacktown police station. There they were greeted by a dozen people on the footpath who called out "mongrels" as they were led inside. Michael Murphy was interviewed in the same room as Les Murphy. Police finished with him at 3.25am. They conducted a second interview about his escape from Silverwater Gaol eight weeks before.

The men were taken on separate run-arounds of the scenes of the crime. The mob on the footpath outside had returned, this time even more numerous than before, and more vicious. Their chant of "Hang the bastards" could be heard upstairs in the Detectives Office. As the police vehicles containing the men arrived back from the run-arounds, the crowd became louder and some people waved placards. One said, "Kill the animals now or they will do it again." Another had, "Wran, rethink the parole system now" and another, "Gaol them for the rest of their natural lives". One woman yelled, "Gas the bastards!"

A telex was sent first to police headquarters, then Australia-wide. Sgt John Marre of the media liaison unit was briefed during the meal break from 7.30 to 8am, and subsequently handled all media conferences and the dozens of phone enquiries about the arrests. He'd been handling many of the media enquiries throughout the investigation. In the office now he noticed an air of relief. "What had impressed me with this team was they were a dedicated group of people, professionals, who had worked so hard together," Marre said. "They were still working on getting the brief together when I arrived there. Kennedy gave me the details and said to me he didn't want to do the interviews, he wanted none of the kudos because it belonged to everyone in that room. He said they'd all been a part of a successful operation. While I was talking I noticed the sound of typing from one of the typewriters behind me had stopped. I looked around and saw the typist, a detective, sound asleep. He'd nodded off while typing a brief."

Outside, amid the chaos, Marre held interview after interview with the media.

Building workers on the roof of the shopping centre across the street from the station lowered two rope nooses. A police sharpshooter was positioned atop another building near the court for fear that a sniper would try to shoot the men. Armed TRG police were positioned in offices around courtroom No.1, where the men were due to appear. Two dozen police closed Kildare Rd, where the station and court are located, in an attempt to control the jeering mob of more than 1500. People jammed the footpaths on either side of the road in front of the court. In case of trouble, police had a back-up team out of sight.

A TV cameraman and a newspaper photographer were perched in trees on the footpath, hoping to get the best vantage point. Businessmen in suits and ties stood and waited, a man in a T-shirt, shorts and thongs read a paper, kids sat in the gutter, while others balanced on fences. Old ladies and retired men joined them while they waited. Some just stood, others looked, many talked. They were all waiting.

One woman walked up to an inspector and held out her hand. "I just want to thank you very much. We all appreciate it," she said. With that a young woman yelled out, "How about three cheers for our police?" The mob joined in immediately, "Hip hooray! hip hooray! hip hooray!" A man called, "I'll give 'em three more cheers if they give the bastards to us!" There was cheering and clapping and laughing.

At 9am the two Murphy brothers appeared in Blacktown Court. Michael Murphy, 33, and Gary Murphy, 28, were charged with murder, abduction, sexual assault and robbery. The court heard Michael Murphy would face a further charge of escaping from Silverwater Gaol on December 27 the previous year. Michael Murphy now had a visible red mark on the side of his face while dry blood was caked on the cheek of his brother. Public solicitor Craig Patrick, who had been hastily summoned to represent the men, told the court the Murphys' facial injuries were the result of "police action" during their arrest. Police prosecutor Sgt Brian Newling told the magistrate that Gary Murphy had attempted to flee when he spotted the police helicopter and was "tackled to the ground and a short struggle ensued". Magistrate Ross McDermid directed the pair be given medical treatment before appearing in Westmead Court later in the morning.

Soon after the Murphys left the court, Mavis Leanne Saunders, 18, of 22 Tari Way, and Debra Jane McAskill, 24, a pensioner of the same address, appeared in the court on charges of being accessories after the murder of Anita Cobby. They were also charged with receiving, assisting, maintaining and harbouring the brothers. The court was told McAskill was the mother of a six-year-old girl and was pregnant with her baby due at any time. Saunders was married to Danny Murphy.

Craig Patrick, also acting for the women, said the pair hadn't surrendered the Murphy brothers to police because they were frightened. Although the Housing Commission home was McAskill's, there was little she could have done when the Murphys arrived to seek refuge, he said. "The defendants were not able to take resolute action and they reacted by some degree of fear." The two women believed the brothers were wanted for a matter in relation to the car they were driving and not murder. He said they had co-operated with police and that the assistance they had given the Murphys had been "very small — one meal . . . no clothes". Sgt Newling said McAskill had not been stopped by the Murphys from leaving the house, having on one occasion taken her child to school. Bail was granted to them on condition they report daily to Campbelltown police and lodge surety of $4000. He ordered them to appear again on March 3. Both women failed to raise the sureties and were taken to Mulawa women's gaol.

Outside the court the crowd was still chanting "Kill! Kill! Kill!" and clapping their hands. Train drivers blasted their horns as they roared past the police station. Some even slowed down to allow passengers to take the opportunity to yell out. Outside the station one Blacktown resident, Margaret Knight, railed to journalists against the soft treatment of molesters and murderers. "They will just be put away for a few years and then released. This is a very cheap price to pay for (taking) a woman's life." Marie Gunning of Penrith protested on behalf of single women living in the area. "I don't even feel safe walking around here in daylight," she said.

As police vehicles carrying the men left Blacktown for Westmead Court, the crowd grew louder, booing and yelling and making throttling motions as the cars, with a police escort, moved away down the street. One Channel 7 news crew persisted with following the troupe, trying to get a shot of Gary Murphy in the back of the police car. The vehicle flew through back streets and around corners to try to lose them and one escort vehicle attempted to block the gap between the two cars. The chase continued for kilometres. Detectives screened their prisoner by putting their arms across the windows. The news crew drew almost alongside the car and the cameraman yelled out, "We only want one shot, mate, and then we'll go." The police car accelerated, leaving the reporters behind, but in all the commotion, Murphy turned around to see what was going on and the crew got their shot.

At Westmead, over 100 jeering Westmead Hospital staff surrounded the police truck carrying Travers, Murdoch and Les Murphy, pounding their fists against it as it proceeded to the court which is inside the hospital grounds. The truck was escorted by two police cars containing TRG police with shotguns drawn and wearing bulletproof vests.

A wire dummy dressed in overalls dangled from a noose on a nearby building and a hand-painted cardboard sign hung under the court sign which read, "Give Anita's killers a free operation (without anaesthetic)." The strictest security was ordered for the court appearances of the men and a metal detector screened everyone who entered the courtroom. A wall of nearly 20 police stood between the charged men and the public benches. Further charges were read, that the three had maliciously inflicted grievous bodily harm on Mrs Cobby with intent to have sexual intercourse without her consent, had abducted her and assaulted her and robbed her of a handbag, purse and clothing on the same date.

Handcuffed and surrounded by TRG officers, the three refused to look at magistrate Derrick Hand. Les Murphy at first would not stand when police prosecutor Sgt Allan Ezzy announced a further charge was to be laid against him for stealing a motor vehicle at Seven Hills on January 28, the car used to abduct Anita Cobby.

It was February 27, John Travers' 19th birthday. Nobody had picked up on it. He would celebrate this birthday rather differently than he had his 18th, when the Travers' fence palings fueled the backyard bonfire. Sharon Travers arrived on the arm of Lisa, her daughter. Dressed in a coral-coloured pinafore with a blue floral blouse underneath, she puffed and panted as she slowly progressed up the footpath to the courtroom doors. She had difficulty making it up the gutter to the footpath because of her bulk. She snarled at the cameramen as they followed her progress. "Do you mind!" she snapped as she passed. "Get that thing out of my face," she said to a cameraman. The press weren't sure who she was but they filmed her as they did most others that day.

Outside the crowd was still yelling. At the end of the two-minute hearing, the three were formally remanded in custody until March 13. The mob howled again when minutes later the older Murphy brothers, remanded from Blacktown court, arrived. Travers, Murdoch and Les Murphy were held in the court cells.

Two more nooses, hung by hospital staff, swung from light poles in Institution Rd, leading to the court building. More signs were placed along the roadside. One read, "Give them what they deserve, not a holiday in prison." As their van approached, the crowd jeered, "Die you mongrels!" and "Hang them!" Dozens of men and women raced to the back of the court where the Murphys were driven into an undercover car park. Roller shutters sealed the car park while the prisoners walked from the vehicles into the back of the court. Peering through tiny holes in the shutters, the people booed and catcalled at the first sight of the men. Cameramen and photographers joined the crowd, also peeping through the small holes to catch a glimpse of the prisoners. The abuse continued as each man stepped from the van.

During their brief appearance, Sgt Ezzy said he would like to put it on record that Gary Murphy received his facial injuries while trying to escape before his arrest. He had been brought down by a tackle and Michael Murphy had been injured while attempting to resist police. Already the Murphy boys had told solicitors they were beaten by police.

John Travers' mother Sharon and sister Lisa and a female companion watched events from behind some cars about 100 metres from the crowd. When the court was adjourned they left in two cars, all in tears.

Angry demonstrators told the media they wanted changes to the prison system. One man, 41-year-old Sergio Volcic of Campbelltown, told them he, too, was a victim of crime. His wife Patricia had been murdered three years earlier at Glenfield, where she worked as a nurse. He was angry that another family had to suffer the anguish he did. "I am here because I strongly feel justice should be seen to be done," Volcic said. "I know exactly what Anita's parents are going through." Nearby a nurse stood holding a sign: "An eye for an eye". The crowd was still gathered at the back of the court and screamed as the men emerged from the doorway to get into the vans.

At midday the investigators returned to the Blacktown police station. On the way in, Speed Kennedy stopped briefly to speak to the press. "Thanks, fellas, for all the help you have given us," and disappeared upstairs. The phones were still ringing. This time with congratulatory messages from hundreds of people. A local publican showed his appreciation. He knew one of the police and threw open his dining room for the team. At 1.30 a group of scruffy police were all smiles in the Sportsman Hotel.

It was March 3 before all the investigators returned to work. By now, the Blacktown police station noticeboard was jammed with cards and letters of congratulation from other police and the public. Premier Wran thanked the men, as did the Police Minister, the local Member of Parliament and other community leaders. They were heroes. However, Speed Kennedy said, "We were still very aware of the lengthy committal proceedings ahead and the loose ends that needed to be tied up."

Just a few days after the first three arrests and amid the euphoria, John Travers' aunt, Miss X, opened a letter. It was unsigned but the envelope had her name and her address on the front. There was a hangman's noose drawn on a piece of paper inside. Her heart pounded as she looked at the drawing. The letter was postmarked Long Bay Gaol, but she had no idea who it was from. It wasn't the first scare she had had in the few days since John Travers had been charged with Anita Cobby's murder. Several death threats had come by telephone. "I was panicking and looking over my shoulder all the time, making sure my kids were alright," she said.

Then she received a letter from Travers. It was covered in faeces. "He promised that, no matter what, he would get me or he would do something horrid to my children," she said. "It was no idle threat and I know that if there was some way he could do it, he would."

By now, Miss X was under 24-hour guard by the Special Weapons Operations Squad, SWOS. After the letters arrived at her house, she was moved to a secret address. "Everyone knew where we lived, everyone involved in the case, so we were easy targets for revenge," she said.

By this time Miss X's family was concerned for her welfare. She regularly kept in touch with them but they were worried when they didn't hear from her."My mother was overseas on a holiday and when she came home and there were no letters from me, she panicked," she said. "I'd left the house and just disappeared and she had no way of contacting me so she feared the worst. She almost reported me missing to police. I didn't know how to explain to her what had happened to me. The SWOS men staying with me asked if they could contact her and sort it out but I had to do it myself. When I rang and told her what I was involved in, she was upset and thought I'd done the murder. She told me she didn't want any more to do with me. But we eventually sorted it out. The whole thing was a shock to her."

Under the strict conditions of the Witness Protection Program, Miss X wasn't allowed to reveal where she was living to anyone, apart from her children and boyfriend. She had to make any contact with other family members and then only on a restricted basis. She didn't have time to say goodbye to friends and they never knew where she went. The children were lectured about revealing where they lived and police explained how important it was for them to keep their silence.

Soon, the TRG police replaced the SWOS men. They could give her specialised care all the time. The SWOS men, an elite squad, were needed for other work. The police, dressed in plain clothes, accompanied them everywhere — when the children were dropped at school, when they shopped, on drives — they never had a moment alone. Miss X remembers the atmosphere was stifling. "I am used to the push and shove of the world, talking to people, having lots of friends, I like people around me. I used to be the sort of person who needed other people around me. I found this new way of life difficult to manage. It was like being under house arrest not being able to go out, and I hated isolation. I know I was very demanding and hard to deal with but the SWOS people were very understanding and would sit and listen to me."

One of the greatest problems, as police saw it, was the emotional strain that being a protected witness placed on Miss X. She was still withdrawing from heroin. She was nervy, irritable, losing weight and not sleeping properly. "I wanted desperately to stick to my methadone program. I'd made that decision myself before all this came up. It was hard. The police supported me fully and I was able to lean on them when times were hard. My minder, John Garvey, was wonderful. I have very special feelings for that man because he was tolerant and understanding. I don't think I would have made it if he hadn't personally put so much time and effort into making me cope. I am very thankful to him from the bottom of my heart."

The changes in her lifestyle left Miss X plenty of time to think. She thought a lot about John Travers. He had told her things to frighten her and other times he had told her things that made her angry. She remembered how she never let him know when these stories affected her because that would have given him satisfaction. Instead, she would push them to the back of her mind. John Travers was always telling her "frightening tales", as she called them. Now they all seemed like portents of his vile act in the Boiler Paddock.

Once he told her what he would do if he killed someone. "John said he would take that person out in the desert, tie them to a tree, do unspeakable things to them and cut them up into little pieces," she said. "'There are lots and lots of little holes out there that go forever and they (his victims) would never be found,' he told me." Now she wondered if Anita Cobby was his only victim.

The five men appeared before Westmead coroner Derrick Hand the week before Easter. A squad of 20 TRG police was on duty that day guarding them on their journey from two gaols, Long Bay and the new Parklea prison near Blacktown. Arrangements were made for traffic lights to be switched off along the routes to the court and police were told to give the vans top priority and "not to stop at any cost".

At the court the prisoners were given another rowdy reception by demonstrators. This time, around 50 people screamed abuse as the prison vans pulled into the back of the court complex. As before, police pulled down the metal roller shutters while the prisoners were unloaded. Again, the crowd pressed hard against the shutters, peering through the tiny holes to catch a glimpse of the men. When they saw them, the mob yelled, "You bastards!" and "Scumbags!" All of the accused were wearing jeans and shirts. Travers walked with his head down. Michael Murphy looked towards the shutters and shouted back at his tormentors. The crowd yelled louder. Then he laughed. Photographers snapped that sneer. The television news screened it, the newspapers printed it. Everyone saw Michael Murphy laugh.

Forty minutes before the court was due to start Garry Lynch arrived, supported on either side by his friend Anne Farmer and her daughter. It would be the first time Garry Lynch came face to face with the men who had killed his daughter. He paused to speak to reporters. "Today is a terrible ordeal for us," he said. "The hardest thing will be seeing the accused when they are in court." That afternoon the Lynchs told journalists they felt relief when they heard of the arrests. Garry Lynch, looking drawn and thin, and his wife, with heavy dark eyes, expressed their gratitude to the police.

Nurses from Westmead Hospital hung a placard from a ground floor window. It read: "Bring back real punishment". Jacqueline Clement, from the group Women Against Violence joined the demonstrators to protest against what she saw as the leniency of the penal system.

Paul McGovern, 24, of Seven Hills started a petition immediately after Anita Cobby's murder calling for the return of capital punishment. Today he was campaigning in person for the cause.

Inside, the accused entered no pleas and their court appearance was over in five minutes. Counsel for Michael Murphy Mr Bill Hosking, QC, asked for a change of venue to a larger court. The matter was adjourned to the Glebe Coroner's Court, in the inner city, on June 23.

Shortly after, Mavis Saunders, Debra McAskill and Ray Paterson appeared, all charged with being accessories after the murder. Saunders faced an additional charge of harbouring.

Chapter 27

Three weeks after the arrest of Gary and Mick Murphy, a diminutive mother of four went to Blacktown police station from her Doonside home. In the three hours Maxine Greensmith was there, she gave police perhaps the most important supporting information of the investigation. It would strengthen the case against the five accused.

Greensmith lived at 6 Tich Place, next door to the Travers' home at No.5. She told police that on the Sunday night Anita Cobby had disappeared she had dinner and a bottle or two of white wine with friends at her home. She was waiting for her boyfriend to come to her house, so whenever a car pulled into their cul-de-sac, she would look outside, thinking it was him. On one of these occasions she noticed a white car pull into the driveway of the Travers home. About 15 minutes later she noticed a second car arrive.

Later, in evidence, Maxine Greensmith said she had known John Travers for some time, also Michael Murdoch, but had only seen Les Murphy around since about the September before. She knew he lived with Lisa in the caravan at the back of the Travers house. She also knew Gary and Michael Murphy by sight, "just to say hi to but not to have a conversation with them".

While her friends were still at her home on the night of Anita Cobby's murder, the neighbour noticed thick smoke coming into her kitchen from the backyard of the house next door. It was just after midnight, she remembered. She went outside to investigate, into the yard, past her above-ground pool, and stood on a pile of dirt to have a better view over the fence. She saw a group of people standing around a fire on the concrete slab in the backyard. Travers and Murdoch were there, so was Les Murphy, Gary Murphy and Michael Murphy and she thought Lisa Travers was there but she wasn't sure. The men were standing around a fire drinking bottles of beer. She noticed the fire made a funny smell, "unlike burning wood", she said. She wasn't happy about the smoke but then again there were so many things about her neighbours that did not please her. It hardly seemed worthwhile complaining.

Later in the week she noticed Travers speaking with Murdoch and the three Murphys in the front yard of his home. And then two weeks later she was woken by police at 6.30am who told her not to worry, they had business in the house next door. Maxine Greensmith said she looked out the window and saw Les Murphy being taken away by police.

That afternoon she had returned home to find Les Murphy in her house, using the telephone. She didn't know who he was talking to but overheard him telling someone the police were trying to pin the Cobby murder on him. He denied being there but went on to graphically detail what he would have done to Anita Cobby if he *had* been present at the murder.

She said Murphy told her that the police were trying to persuade him to have a blood test and be hypnotised. She asked him if he was going to do it. Murphy replied, "No way." She told him if he had nothing to hide he should go and have the test and he told her, "You know what the pigs are like, they'll try to pin it on us . . . no way! I'm going to piss off." He then told her: "You know that I never went out that night, the car didn't go out that night and if the car doesn't go out, I don't go out." Maxine Greensmith replied that she didn't remember exactly but she thought Murphy insisted, "You tell the Ds that the car never went out that night and I was home."

She said after that she began to get regular calls from people for Les Murphy. They were using her number to contact him. The callers were always males.

Maxine Greensmith said this reminded her of another incident which convinced her to go to the police. In the month before the murder, her 13-year-old daughter Kelly-Ann ran crying into the house, upset about what she had seen over the fence in the Travers yard. Maxine Greensmith looked out the back window and saw John Travers kneeling over a lamb. Its throat had been cut and blood was flowing from its neck. Travers held the struggling animal's head back and she watched as he cut the animal's stomach with a knife. Sickened, she had to turn away. The events took on new meaning after

Travers and his mates had been charged with the brutal slaying.

The murder of Anita Cobby provoked unprecedented outrage across the nation. Public servant Paul McGovern, campaigning hard for the return of capital punishment, said, "Before this case I didn't support capital punishment but now I totally agree. There is something wrong with our penal system when a woman can't walk safely down a road and the men who commit terrible crimes are kept with three square meals a day and all the luxuries of home. They should be made to pay for a life with a life." Within a week he had collected nearly 5000 signatures of people demanding the reintroduction of capital punishment. McGovern didn't know Anita Cobby or the Lynch family but this was beside the point. The petition snowballed. "I started getting offers of help from people who wanted to collect names too. People from all over Sydney added their support." After six weeks, McGovern had nearly 20,000 signatures. In April he presented them to NSW Opposition Leader Nick Greiner who passed them on to the Premier. Later, a TV viewers' poll conducted by Channel TEN found an astounding 92.8 percent of the 15,470 callers were in favour of the reintroduction of the death penalty.

The Lynch family

Anita Lorraine Lynch, a happy childhood in a happy home.

Left: Anita, her mother Grace's pride and joy.

Below: Anita and John Cobby on their wedding day.

Right: Always a lover of the outdoors, Anita is pictured with pet dog Lucy.

The Lynch family

News Ltd

Left: Being crowned Miss Western Suburbs in 1979 gave Anita the confidence to be a model.

Above: At a charity function with NSW Premier Wran.

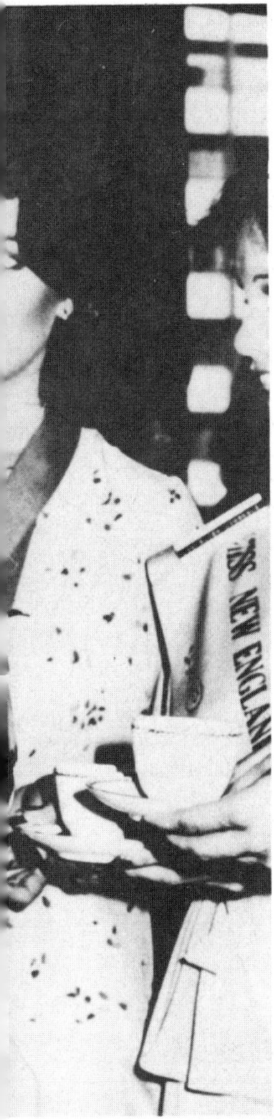

News Ltd

John Fairfax and Sons

Above: Garry Lynch, Anita's father, faced his ordeal with dignity, strength and courage.

Below: At Anita's funeral. Garry and Grace Lynch, daughter Kathryn and her husband Ray.

News Ltd

John Fairfax and Sons

Above: The manhunt begins. Police comb the area around Reen Rd, Prospect, where the body of Anita Cobby was found earlier that day.

Right: Constable Debbie Wallace, wearing clothes similar to Anita Cobby's, re-enacts her last journey from Central station to Blacktown in the hope of jogging passengers' memories. Det Graham Rosetta is at right.

News Ltd

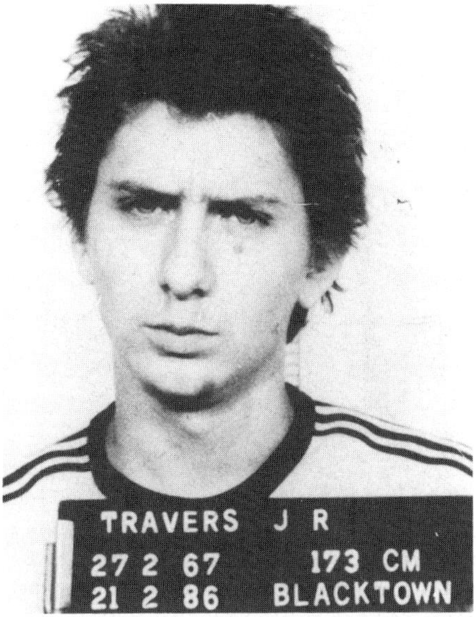

John Fairfax and Sons

The official police photograph of John Travers, taken shortly after his arrest.

Below: Soon after his arrest, a handcuffed Michael Murphy accompanied Detectives Raue (left) and Kennedy to the Boiler Paddock, scene of Anita Cobby's murder.

Above: Detectives Raue, Heskett and Waters with Les Murphy by the incinerator slab in Travers' backyard. Below: Detectives Kennedy, Raue and Heskett take Michael Murphy on a run-around.

Above: SWOS police close in on Gary and Michael Murphy.

Below: Det Raue takes the Murphys away after the Tari Way raid.

News Ltd

Above: The diminutive Les Murphy in custody.

Above centre: John Travers under heavy guard at his mother's funeral

Right: Michael Murphy is led to a police van for charging.

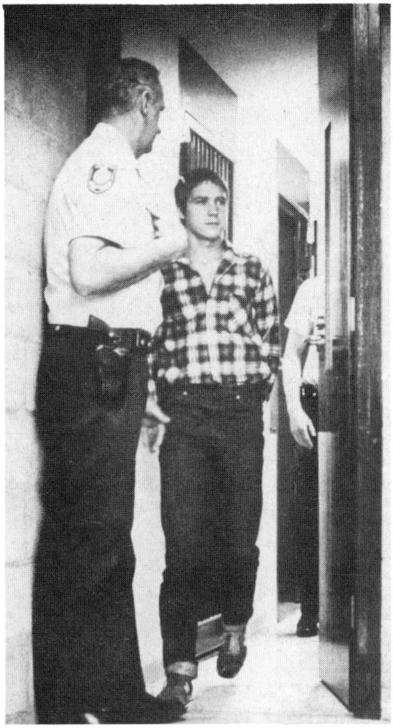

News Ltd

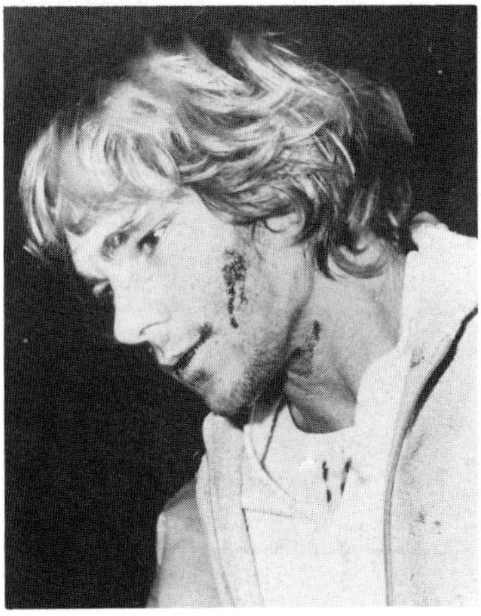

News Ltd

Above: Michael Murdoch under police escort.

Left: A bloodied Gary Murphy after being tackled and apprehended by police during the raid at Tari Way, Glenfield.

News Ltd

Above: A furious mob calls for the blood of the accused as they are transported to Blacktown police station.

Right: NSW Opposition Leader Nick Greiner with a petition signed by 10,000 western suburbs citizens demanding the death penalty for the Cobby killers.

John Fairfax and Sons

John Fairfax and Sons

An emotional Garry and Grace Lynch are beseiged by the media after the men charged with their daughter's murder are found guilty.

News Ltd

John Fairfax and Sons

Far left: Distraught friends of Les Murphy protest his innocence after the guilty verdict.

Left: Elated bus driver Jackson Mashinini rushes from the courtroom to announce that the guilty men had received life sentences.

Above: Police and prosecutors reward themselves with a well-earned drink after the guilty verdict. From left: Det Rosetta, Det Waters, Det Rynne, solicitor Jenny Betts, Crown prosecutor Alan Saunders, QC, Det Kennedy, Det O'Toole and Det Raue.

News Ltd

Anita Cobby at rest. "Her Light Shines Forever".

Chapter 28

The fury directed at the men charged with killing Anita Cobby still ran strong five months after their arrests when committal proceedings began. Police took every precaution. In a move that was rare in Sydney courts, all members of the public and the media had to pass through metal detectors and then be searched by a hand-held electronic scanner before being allowed into the courtroom. The reason was two-fold: to protect the five men from the public, and to protect the witnesses, particularly Miss X. On the opening day of the hearing, police scoured nearby rooftops with tracker dogs looking for anyone or anything that could threaten the safety of those in the court.

On most days during the hearing, 19 police, including six members of the TRG squad, were assigned to secure the courthouse building on busy Parramatta Rd in Glebe. At different times, up to 10 uniformed police stood guard inside the courtroom. Several were stationed at the rear of the building to keep an eye on photographers, cameramen and journalists battling for exclusive shots of the accused.

Committal proceedings are held to test the bare bones of the prosecution case, to determine whether the matter should proceed. Each accused man applied to have his case heard separately but this was denied. The five sat in steel-framed chairs barely a metre from the public gallery. In front, their solicitors sat around a huge wooden table, which took up most of the room. At one end sat the prosecutor, Sgt Ezzy.

The five wore jeans, sandshoes and casual shirts. They smirked at each other. Travers' cold, unsettling eyes seemed dead, registering no emotion.

The media acknowledged but kept its distance from Grace and

Garry Lynch, leaving them to their privacy. "We were surprised to see them there being so brave and facing the men who were supposed to have killed their daughter," remembered television reporter Norm Lipson. "I guess we just respected their private grief."

For the first time, family members of the men faced the Lynchs. It was uncomfortable for both. Danny Murphy approached Grace and Garry. He stumbled over his words, offering his condolences and help, wondering if there was anything he could do. There wasn't. Rose Murdoch and Grace Lynch found themselves both in the ladies room on one occasion. It was a strain. Later, Rose Murdoch told Grace and Garry how sorry she was about what had happened to Anita.

Many of the police involved in the investigation who had had little contact with the Lynchs now came to know them. The detectives were protective of the family and Speed Kennedy warned them when a section of forensic evidence, outlining their daughter's horrific injuries, would be given in court. He advised them not to sit in. Grace waited outside for one section of it but Garry chose to be present while Dr Malouf gave his findings. An acquaintance of Anita, Kerrie Sandberg, ran crying from the courtroom when Malouf described how one of three incisions in Anita's neck had cut into her spinal column, exposing her vertebrae. Garry Lynch dropped his head, shook it and blinked back tears. This time Grace was not at his side to hold his hand.

Aided by Paul Hamilton's photos, Dr Malouf first described the scene in the Boiler Paddock and later gave details of the postmortem. These photos were harrowing but they were fact. There was much legal argument about them — whether they were too explicit to be displayed in a court and perhaps later to be viewed by a jury and whether the colour photographs were too emotive. The media and the public craned their necks to snatch glimpses of them while they were passed around the bar table for examination and then up to the magistrate. Every photo received the same grim reaction.

Dr Malouf told the court he found Anita Cobby had died from loss of blood after her head had been almost severed from her neck. He told the court he believed she was conscious at the time of the cut and it would have taken approximately two minutes for her to die. There were three major lacerations running from the left side of the neck to behind the right ear. The largest was 30cm long. There were also three minor cuts across her throat. "The cuts were jagged in parts and clean-edged in other places and that suggests a very sharp instrument," he said. "The jaggedness suggests drawing of the instrument across the structures of the neck." The scientific photos portrayed them as gaping holes, each separated by a fine strand of skin. At one point, where there was no more skin to slice the cuts then ran into each other. "One laceration, cut on the right side of the neck, completely destroyed all tissues, muscles, nerves, arteries and veins . . ." Dr Malouf said. ". . . there were quite extensive contusions on the head, on the breasts, on the face, on the shoulders, on the groin and on the legs," Dr Malouf said. There was a 12cm wound on her back and small lacerations on her legs, consistent with nicks from contact with a barbed wire fence. Her anus was lacerated, there was a graze on her breast. Both eyes, left thigh and leg and left arm were bruised and there were fractures to her hand, defence wounds, Dr Malouf said, caused when Anita lifted her left hand to stop the knife bearing down on her throat. The photographs showed that her left hand had been sliced so hard by the blade of the knife, two of her fingers had been opened to the bone. The cuts to her middle finger ran nearly the entire length to the knuckle. The top joint was almost severed by the force. Dr Malouf confirmed that Anita Cobby was menstruating at the time of the attack.

He said blood tests had been positive on Travers' jeans, singlet, joggers and laces as well as on a small brown-handled knife in a sheath, a bayonet-type knife, a large Rambo-style knife, a wooden-handled knife and a black-handled butcher's knife, all belonging to Travers. A pair of jeans of Murdoch were tested for bloodstains. All the items returned positive to blood but the tests were inconclusive as to whether the blood was human or animal and what blood group it belonged to.

There was much legal argument about the Rambo-style knife that was produced in court. The prosecution wanted the knife accepted in evidence because it was similar to the one used to kill Anita Cobby. Defence lawyers argued against it being accepted as an exhibit because it was not *the* knife. The murder knife was never recovered but, aided by descriptions and drawings from Travers and Murdoch, one identical to the murder weapon was purchased by police at the same archery shop in Parramatta where Travers had bought the original.

The McGaugheys were called to give their account of the abduction and subsequent search. They were followed by John Reen, the dairy farmer who discovered the body.

The police's surprise weapon was Miss X. She was the key to the prosecution case. But there was a battle to have her taped conversations with Travers and Murdoch accepted as evidence. Legal argument centred around the tapes' admissability on the grounds that the recordings were made secretly by police and on whether the Supreme Court warrant, obtained by telephone, was in fact legally binding. Hours and hours of debate over the tapes was conducted behind closed doors. Only the police and the legal people were directly involved. Finally it was agreed most of the tapes' contents should be heard.

Miss X was terrified about appearing in court. "I had never been in a courtroom before. I didn't know what to expect, so to prepare myself I went up there a few weeks before the hearing to check it out and see what it looked like." She tried desperately to control her fear of walking into the courtroom to confront the five accused men. She knew now she had done the right thing in helping bring Travers to justice. She was certain of that. "But I didn't want to face them in court," she said. "I really didn't want to. It's pretty hard to destroy somebody. But John had done wrong and that was that. He'd committed murder so he'd have to pay for it".

Chapter 29

When Miss X first stepped into the witness box at the committal proceedings the media was present in force with notebooks, court cameras and tape recorders. There were strangers everywhere. There were barristers and solicitors using words she strained to understand, trying to unsettle her and cast doubt on her statements. She barely noticed the three familiar figures of Ian Kennedy, Graham Rosetta and Kevin Raue sitting two metres from her. She was emotionally overwhelmed by having to go back over every detail of her involvement.

Worst of all there was Travers, Murdoch and the three Murphy brothers to contend with. "They were just a metre or so in front of me," she remembered. "That was so uncomfortable. When I first sat down in the witness box I thought I was going to faint. I looked straight at them. They mouthed obscenities at me. They all glared but then they looked away. The eldest Murphy listened quite well, he paid attention," Miss X said.

The defence fired all its ammunition at her. They claimed she was motivated by greed, deceiving the men to help police so as to secure the $100,000 reward offered by the State Government for the conviction of the Cobby killers. She strenuously denied this, pointing out she hadn't even put in a claim. But she was hurt by the accusation. "It seemed so unfair."

Then the defence raised her drug habit. She admitted she had once had a drug problem but now she was on the methadone program and had been for five months before she became mixed up in this. She was ashamed of her addiction, something her mother, even today, doesn't know about. But she is proud of the fact she was able to beat drugs. "Yes, I was an addict and a fairly bad one," she said. "The defence's questions upset me, not because I wanted to hide it but because I couldn't see the relevance of mentioning my addiction in court."

She had first come into contact with drugs in mid-1979 when she arrived in Sydney with her husband and six-month-old child. She had no friends in Sydney. She was only 20 when her husband left her. "It was difficult because I didn't want to go home," she said. "My family was unhappy about me marrying so young — I was only 17. When my marriage broke up I was too proud to go home snivelling to Mum. I really wanted to make things work out. Some very kind people took me in and looked after me. But I came into contact with drugs here for the first time. The son in the house was a user." The son was John Travers' uncle and the house was Travers' grandmother's.

"It scared me at first," Miss X remembered. "But then I saw him happy and laughing and drugs seemed an easy way to cope with my own problems. Mentally, I was having a hard time so I gave heroin a try and it did make it easier to deal with things. I kept going, using more frequently until I had to have it all the time. I couldn't survive without a hit. To get it, I dealt. I didn't do burglaries and I didn't work the streets . . . And then I wanted help so I got on a methadone program."

It was hard to stick to the program but she knew she had to. Even so, the events of the past months had made her question whether beating drugs was worth all the pain. She could have used some comfort now.

She found the courtroom questioning about her drug habit emotionally draining but she bit her lip and kept going. Deep down she was proud she had kept off the stuff for nearly a year despite the turmoil her life was in.

Nothing could have prepared her for her ordeal in court. "The thing that really upset me was seeing the exhibits on a table in front of me. John's jeans. They were my boyfriend's and he had given them to John. I had bought them myself. I cut the holes in the hips for John because he was a little thicker. They were the ones John wore on the night of the murder. Seeing them there upset me more than anything."

After Miss X stepped down from the witness box at the front of the courtroom, having finished her evidence, there was an adjournment. As the prisoners stood, single file, ready to leave the court through a side door, Kevin Raue noticed Travers watching Miss X intently. Speed Kennedy noticed him too. Without a word, the pair moved from their spot beside the men and stood directly in front of her, blocking Travers' line of vision. Travers suddenly took three quick steps forward and lunged at her. "You bitch, you fuckin' bitch. I'll get you," he snarled. Shocked, Miss X took a step back, standing stunned behind Kennedy and Raue. Other officers immediately crowded around the prisoners and Miss X. Now sandwiched between four policemen, Travers was marched out. Miss X's eyes stung with tears. She recalled, "That was really terrifying. I had to walk right beside them all in the court. I almost brushed shoulders with them. Of course there were police all around but there wasn't very much distance between them and me."

Later in proceedings, Michael Murphy and Travers were talking to each other, lightheartedly smiling and shrugging their shoulders. This so infuriated television journalist Norm Lipson that he jumped to his feet, muttering to his colleagues he was "going to punch that Travers' lights out. Doesn't he realise this is a serious matter!" After being calmed by two colleagues Lipson was cautioned by a court official.

After four days of evidence and amid unprecedented media attention, each of the five accused was found to have a case to answer for the murder of Anita Cobby.

The horror of their daughter's death had been brought painfully back to the Lynchs during the proceedings. While they outwardly seemed to be handling the pressure, they now needed to get away for a break, a holiday so they could clear their minds and prepare themselves for the trial six months later.

The months between the committal proceedings and the trial proved hard days for Miss X. Her life had been turned upside down and she felt like a caged animal. Now, after surviving the proceedings, she knew what to expect in court but realised it wouldn't get any easier. She hated the prospect of what she would still have to face. She again started to question whether she had done the right thing in getting involved in this whole affair.

Her children were being unsettled by all the publicity and the police guard on their home. Added to that was the burden that they all cared for somebody who had done a terrible thing. "The children had nightmares and started bedwetting," Miss X said. "They couldn't understand how a person close to them, someone they loved, could kill another person." She dreamed of normalcy in their lives.

Again and again she replayed the whole chain of events in her mind. Other incidents involving John cropped up all the time. "I thought of all the horrible things he had done, his violence with animals, his terrorising of women. He told me about the rapes, about the things he would do. He was trying to terrorise me with his stories because he enjoyed dominating me. I really couldn't cope with these stories but I never let him see." She discussed her innermost feelings with Travers' uncle, her de facto husband. Then each time she came to the same conclusion: she *was* doing the right thing. Soon this ordeal would be over, leaving her free and with a clear conscience.

Maxine Greensmith, too, after her damning evidence, was put on the Witness Protection Program. She was moved out of her Tich Place home and was relocated by the Housing Commission. Her house was upgraded, it was bigger and brick this time. They also helped her out with a washing machine and other essentials. But she felt isolated from her family and cut off from the world. "I had no identity," Maxine Greensmith said. "I couldn't use my real name and I had to wait for some time before another one was given to me. Simple things like cashing a pension cheque became a nightmare because I had no ID with my new name on it. It upset the kids and I was a nervous wreck."

Then she, too, started to receive death threats. "Very early one morning I received a phone call. The caller said he would kill me. I froze. I asked him how he knew where I was. My new telephone number was silent. He hung up. I had to go through the process of changing it all again. It was like a horror story."

Chapter 30

The day of the trial arrived, cool and sunny. March 16, 1987, one year and 40 days since Anita Cobby was found dead in the Prospect paddock.

The Supreme Court complex at Darlinghurst, East Sydney, is one of Australia's oldest. It is a grand building with sandstone columns, a miniature Parthenon. It has a manicured lawn in front of a curving driveway, blocked by huge wrought-iron gates at either end. This day, the first day of what was being called Australia's murder trial of the century, only judges, select barristers, elite police and some court officials were allowed entry to the grounds of the court. Just one journalist was granted a parking space. Joe Morris, a veteran from the Sydney *Daily Telegraph* was almost an institution at the Darlinghurst court. It had been his beat for years and he had reported on many big trials held there. He was semi-retired now and in his 70s but still kept an eye on the court rounds. He was neat and wore a '50s-style checked hat which he tipped to every lady. Joe showed the younger fellows what chivalry is all about by taking the elbow of female journalists as they walked down steps or through uneven patches of footpath. One of Joe's trademarks was his rough sheets of notepaper. Never was he seen to use a notebook, always square sheets of loose paper, thought by many to be leaves from the paper towel rack in the men's room.

Darlinghurst courtroom No.5 looked the part. The court with its huge steel doors stands in the centre of the building. Inside it is old-fashioned with polished wooden benches, high ceiling and fortress-like dock in the centre. The desk tops make fascinating reading and record decades of court cases through the names of police, journalists and criminals all carved into the wood. Included among the hundreds of names are "George Jones, Baker-Crump-Lamb-

Morse murder trial 1974", "R.G. Stewart, News, 1928", "Brian Hogben, Mirror, 1942", who went on to become editor of that paper, "Jeff McMullen, ABC" and even "Clark Kent, Daily Planet".

At 9.30am, half an hour before the court was due to begin, a crowd milled outside. More people were there than seats inside to accommodate them. On the footpath, a small group of demonstrators held a peaceful protest with home-made signs. There were only eight of them, a far cry from the angry mob scenes at the first court appearances of the accused men.

Metal detectors were used again to screen people entering the courtroom. Security officers ran hand-held scanners over everyone wishing to enter the court. And all were asked to empty their pockets and remove belts, coins, keys, watches, cigarette packs and anything that carried metal or foil before they walked through the detector. Women had to open their bags and remove metal nail files and aerosol cans, leaving them on a makeshift laminex table in front of the court door. They were returned on the way out. It was the first time many of the journalists had encountered such strict security. Guards patrolled the grounds and extra court staff were rostered for the duration of the trial.

The trial judge was 63-year-old Justice Alan Maxwell, a quiet, eminent judge who had been on the bench for 13 years. He had presided over a sequence of celebrated court cases in 1980, only a few months after the killing of Sydney Family Court judge David Opas. Security in the form of extra guards was tightened on Justice Maxwell's home that year after reports of shotgun fire close to where he lived. At the time he was the judge on the so-called "Croatian Six" bomb conspiracy trial.

Minutes before proceedings began word spread that one of the men would plead guilty. Everyone tried to guess which one of the defendants it was, and then John Travers admitted his guilt. He announced he had cut Anita Cobby's throat and would not contest it. The Lynchs were shocked but relieved.

Travers stood in the dock as the charges against him were read out. Murder, kidnapping, sexual assault, inflicting grievous bodily harm with intent to have sexual intercourse, assault and robbery of Mrs Cobby's handbag and clothing, and stealing a motor vehicle. Justice Maxwell asked Travers if he knew the maximum penalties for the crimes, particularly for murder. "Are you fully aware of what these charges are that you are pleading guilty to?" Without emotion, Travers replied, "Yes, Your Honour." Justice Maxwell remanded him for sentencing at the end of the trial and ordered he be kept in strict custody. None of the other four looked up at Travers or spoke to him as he was led away. He disappeared down the steep flight of wooden stairs in the floor behind their seats in the dock, to the cells underneath the courtroom. They all believed it would be the last time they would be together.

A group of 400 people had been called up from whom a pool of potential jurors would be called. The idea was to give lawyers a good cross section of the community to choose from. Juror selection this day was a long and tedious task. After four hours, eight men and four women were sworn in.

In the early afternoon, Justice Maxwell spoke to the jury before the opening addresses from the Crown and the defence counsellors began. His Honour was an elderly man with square metal glasses and fair skin, thin lips, thick bushy eyebrows and fine silver hair hidden under his wig. He looked learned and distinguished in his red gown. He told the jurors not to be swayed or influenced by anything they may read in the press, hear on the radio or see on television. They had to judge the case on what they heard in sworn evidence from the witness box, discarding any rumour or anything learned from outside the courtroom.

The Crown prosecutor, Alan Saunders, a Queens Counsel, read at length from statements the four remaining accused, Michael, Gary and Les Murphy and Michael Murdoch, allegedly gave to police after their arrests. Looking straight at the jury, Saunders animatedly told how Anita Cobby had been brutally and savagely murdered. He said she was still conscious when her throat was cut after she had been dragged into a car, stripped, beaten, robbed and repeatedly raped. The evidence, he said, would show she had been killed so she could not identify her attackers. Above his head he waved a long-bladed hunting knife which, he said, was similar to the one used to kill the nursing sister. "You would be less than human if you are not horrified by what you will hear in the trial," he said. "That will be your natural reaction . . . We will prove beyond reasonable doubt the guilt of the accused."

During the address Grace Lynch, dressed in a pale blue skirt-suit, sat at the back of the court with Anne Farmer, her face impassive. Garry Lynch waited in the witness room. He was the trial's first witness and his evidence was brief, confirming he was Anita Cobby's father. When he told the court he was the one who had identified her body at the morgue, his voice momentarily broke. A wave of sympathy flooded the room.

He stood less than five metres from where the prisoners were sitting. He too, appeared composed, his hands resting lightly on top of the wooden stand behind which he stood to give his evidence. Of the accused, only Les Murphy continually watched Garry Lynch. Michael and Gary Murphy quietly spoke with each other and Murdoch kept his head bowed most of the time. At the conclusion of his evidence, Garry Lynch asked Justice Maxwell, "May I join my wife at the back of the court?" and, after receiving a nod of assent from His Honour, sat in the public gallery.

During that first day, Michael Murphy made many notes in a folder and constantly spoke to Gary Murphy, explaining things to him because, his solicitor explained later, Murphy had impaired hearing and was having difficulty picking up the evidence.

Joe Morris sat with the other journalists in the old wooden press gallery. He had seen many accused men in this court over the years. He eyed each of these as they sat in the dock and, on the way out, whispered to a colleague, "They're no good, not one of them. They ought to lock 'em up and throw away the key."

The following morning brought a sensation. Justice Maxwell had barely taken his seat when Bill Hosking, QC, jumped to his feet claiming a grave injustice to his client, Michael Murphy. There was a murmur throughout the courtroom. Murphy, he said, had been "gravely prejudiced" in a newspaper report that described his client in a way that was "evidence of a bad character of a devastating kind". The ensuing debate was heard in the absence of the jury. Hosking told how after court the previous day, he had bought a copy of *The Sun* from a newspaper stand 20 or 30 metres from the court and saw an article which mentioned that Michael Murphy was an escapee. He said it was "more than likely the members of the jury purchased the same newspaper . . ." so learning of Murphy's background. Justice Maxwell agreed, Michael Murphy couldn't have a fair trial. The suggestion that he had been in gaol and had a prior record could cause prejudice against him. The jury, he said, could be poisoned. Lawyers for the other men argued their clients could be perceived as "tarred with the same brush" and the jury could no longer be impartial. Saunders said he too was "horrified and gravely concerned" about the article's effect on the jury. Justice Maxwell adjourned the court briefly then called the jury back and said he acted "with great reluctance . . . but as a result I have no other alternative but to discharge you." The trial was aborted.

Everyone was shocked. The media was stunned. It was rare for a newspaper to cause a trial to be aborted, let alone the trial of the century. *The Sun* had three journalists covering the trial, a court reporter, a police roundsman and a feature writer. Which had blundered? The problem was that in police descriptions of the man during the investigations, police had released the information that Michael Murphy was an escapee. So it was generally known already, but not allowed to be published or broadcast. Later a radio journalist admitted he also noted the fact in a report on the opening day, but luckily he wasn't singled out for attention. Max Fitzgibbon, a senior journalist with 30 years reporting experience, realised his was the offending story. He immediately apologised to Speed Kennedy and the other police, the Crown and defence lawyers. It was an honest mistake and his colleagues rallied to his support. After all, it had gone through five experienced newspaper staff for checking, including a sub-editor, the chief sub and the newspaper editor, before it hit the streets.

Justice Maxwell set the new trial down for a week later, March 23, because of the difficulties of calling another jury pool at short notice.

So it all started again the following week with a new jury. Garry Lynch repeated his evidence. John Reen, the farmer who had found Anita's body in the paddock, told the court how he had alerted police. He was the second of 43 Crown witnesses to give evidence. Linda and Paul McGaughey explained how both had heard the screams and saw a woman dragged into a car and how their brother had gone searching for her. Dr Joseph Malouf gave the post-mortem results.

On the third day, Const Paul Hamilton's vivid colour photographs of the murder victim once again brought howls of protest from the bar table. After the jury had seen several of the photographs, Bill Hosking objected to the colour prints being handed to the jury, telling Justice Maxwell, "They are unduly horrific, enough is enough." Later, Hosking objected again, saying, "Their cumulative effect is quite extraordinary." And later still he attacked the use of the photos, "The Crown has presented a highly selective and prejudiced selection of photos." The objections were overruled one after the other and more than 100 of the colour photos as well as black and white prints of the murder scene and the five men on their run-arounds, were passed silently and quickly around the seven men and five women jurors. (The jury was reduced to 11 people when one juror fell ill in the first week.)

By now police had been living in Miss X's home for a year. Protecting her remained a top priority. Her evidence was vital if a conviction was to be secured against the accused. She was scared, shaking still, and she had lost weight. But she was determined to see this through.

In the witness box she would shake and sometimes cry. But she was a strong witness. She told of her first visit to the cells in Blacktown police station where John Travers was being held. In her police statement, taken after the visit, she had said: "I spoke to John through the opening in the door. The first thing I said to him was, 'Why have they got you here?' John said, 'They're trying to pin that murder on me.' I took hold of his hand and put it to my face and I said, 'Did you do it?' I started crying. He started to cry and he said, 'Yes.' I said, 'John, you don't go near the railway station, how did you get her?' He said, 'She was walking up the street and we grabbed her and got her in the car.'

"I said, 'Who else was with you?' He said, 'Les.' I said, 'Who's Les? I don't know Les.' He said, 'Lisa's boyfriend.' He said, 'Gary, Mick.' I said, 'Mick Murdoch?' He said, 'No, Les' two brothers. Gary and Mick *and* Mick Murdoch.' I said, 'Is that all?' He said, 'Yes.'

"I said, 'Does anybody else know?' And he said, 'No.' I said, 'What can I do to help you?' He said, 'Go home and get the knife with the brown wooden handle out of the kitchen drawer.' I said, 'Is that what you used?' He said, 'Yeah.' John said, 'Get the jeans, the ones that were Mr X's, they're really faded, they've got slits in the waistband. They're somewhere at home.' I said, 'What else?' He said, 'The dark blue tank top, it's at Mrs McNee's (Miss X's washing lady). I said, 'No it's not. It's at my place. She gave it to me on the Friday after you got picked up.' I said, 'What did you have on your feet?' He said, 'I've got them here (indicating a pair of running shoes). I washed them once.' I told him he'd better wash them again. He said, 'They've taken the laces.' I said, 'What about her things?' He said, 'We took them home and burnt them in the incinerator, the concrete block. Then we took the ashes to the dump. But still check the incinerator.'

"I said, 'What about the car, where's that? Did you get rid of that properly?' He said, 'We burnt it. Go to Les, he'll tell you where it is. Get Mr X and get rid of it, put it in the river or something. Fucking Mick (Murdoch), he's told them all about it (the car). I told the pigs that we dumped the car and told Les that he could have the wheels. After you find the car, leave Les and the others out of it, 'cause if they get picked up they might not be strong enough to hold.'

"He told me that he wrote a letter yesterday to his mum. The desk sergeant had it and John told me, 'Get the letter and take it to Mum and tell her (to say to police) that on the night (of the murder) she went to bed and I was there (at home) and when she woke up I was still there.' John told me, 'Tell Les, Gary and Mick to stay away from Paterson.' I said, 'Who's Paterson?' He said, 'That's where the car was painted. He's a dog, a dobber, tell them to keep away from him.'

"John then said, 'Tell Gary and Mick to be at the back of here (he pointed to the back of the police station) with a couple of shotties (shotguns) between 3 and 3.30 in the morning before I go to court. It's only a skeleton crew at that time. The oldest bloke has got the keys. They don't check on me when the sun's up, during the night about four times.' When he mentioned the couple of shotties he also said, 'to bust me out'. He said, 'If they nail me, I'll take the rap for everyone, so they owe me.'

"'You've gotta watch Mick Murdoch, he's got bail and he's doing it for the money.' I said, 'What money?' He said, 'The hundred thousand (the reward money).' He also told me that one of the fellows involved was 'on the run'. He said, 'He's escaped and he's on the run.' He was talking about the Mick who is Les' brother.

"He also mentioned a guy named Terry from the CYSS at St Mary's. He helped him with some sort of CYSS program once." Miss X remembered that program. John was on probation on the condition he work with this church group. "He had really conned the court into letting him get involved in this group," Miss X recalled. "The poor fellow (Terry) thought he could help John and John took part in making a video with the group, talking to reformed kids about their days of crime. I remember after he'd made it he begged me to go and see them and stop the bit he'd filmed. He was so scared that all the girls he'd hurt — raped — would recognise him now from his teardrop tattoo. When I told him I couldn't he seriously considered cutting the teardrop out with a knife."

The video, designed for sale as a home video, was made by the Catholic Audio Visual Centre at Homebush. It dealt with troubled teenagers. In it, John Travers talked about housebreaking, likening himself to a modern day Robin Hood, robbing the rich. He considered himself the poor. "The people that have everything don't look at the people who have nothing," he said. "They think that their dog's got a broken toenail, they think that's the misery of their whole life. They don't look at the other people that have to struggle . . . If I went and done a house or something and I saw that the people were living on bare necessities, I wouldn't take nothing. I'd just walk straight out the door again. I don't do poor areas. I go to a rich area . . . Probably they're all insured, it's not going to hurt them anyway. They'll probably claim more insurance. Yeah, that's what I'd say, just thinking of the richer for the poorer . . . like Robin 'ood. But I don't give it out 'cause I don't get enough."

The discovery of that video by *The Sun* newspaper after the trial and its subsequent screening on TV prompted a fierce protest from the Catholic Church. Father Brian Lucas, spokesman for the Church, said the video had been withdrawn from sale as soon as it was realised Travers had been charged with the Cobby murder. Lucas was critical of the media, for the "exploitation of Mr Travers' privacy".

The second statement Miss X gave in court was made to police after she had been to see Les Murphy at Travers' request.

Miss X and her boyfriend, Mr X, had driven to the Travers' home in Doonside around 5.45pm. "Lisa Travers introduced me to Les who I had not previously met and I said, 'Les, I'd like to speak with you please, can we go somewhere to talk?' and I started to walk towards the front of the house, but he said, 'No, no, not out the front, in the back.' We walked through the kitchen to the back of the house in the yard and I said, 'I've been to see John.' He said, 'How is he?' I said, 'Holding up. John told me to come and see you, you've got to tell me where the car is.' Les said, 'I don't know.' I said, 'You've got to know.' He said, 'We've got to get rid of it'. Les said, 'They've been to me Mum's looking for me, they're trying to get us for that murder.' I said, 'Never mind about that, we've got to have the car. How can we find it? Do your brothers know where it is?' He said, 'I don't know.' I said, 'Can you ring them?' He said, 'Not really but I'll try.' I said, 'Come on then, don't tell anyone else, just come.'

"We walked back through the house to the car and Les got some two bob bits and Lisa got in the car. We drove to a phone box in Hillend Rd, and Les said, 'I'll ring my sister and leave a message with her for them to contact me straight away.' He made one telephone call while I sat in the car. It appeared to be a bad connection, he was yelling into the phone and he repeated what she was saying to him. I could hear him say, 'Down Powers Rd, right on Owens and left on Plumpton. It's opposite the blue car.' He said to the person on the telephone, 'Can you come over in half an hour? Okay I'll see you then.' He got back in the car and Les said, 'My sister wants me to go and stay with them at Granville.' Mr X said to him, 'Can you tell us what's going on, what's it all about?' Les said, 'They're trying to get the five of us for that murder.' I said, 'What do you mean? You, your brothers, Mick and John for the murder?' He said, 'Yeah.'

"At that time we were in Plumpton Rd. He said, 'There's the blue car over there, it (the grey car) is gone.' We pulled up and had a look and he said, 'Hang on, the people around the corner have a lot of Holdens, we'll have a look there.' We drove around the corner to a house with a lot of wrecks in the yard but Les said, 'It's not there. The cops said it was green but it wasn't, it was grey.' We went back to near where the car was dumped and Les told Mr X, 'Make up a story that your wife's (sic) car was stolen and that you just found out it was dumped here. Ask that bloke if he knows what happened.' Mr X got out and spoke to a chap, came back to the car and said, 'Yes, an H something (I can't remember) was burning the night he moved in. A couple of days later it disappeared. It had those orange stickers slapped on it.'

"We left and drove back to Tich Place. I said to Les, 'We've got to find the car, it's gotta go John said.' Les said, 'It's either at the dump or a wrecker's got it. Can I stay with you and we'll go to the dump and look for it?' I said, 'I don't think that's a good idea. Mr X and I can say we're just snooping, but you're wanted. Go home and wait till we ring you or come round. I forgot — John said you must stay away from Paterson.' Les said, 'I know, he's a dobber.' Les directed us to a street behind where he lives, we dropped him off and I saw him climb a fence and we drove away."

The court also heard the conversation Miss X had with Travers on the second visit to his cell, the confession secretly taped by the hidden recorder. In it Travers talked about the daring escape he had planned. He asked Miss X if she could still "get them passports from Kerry?"

"Did you get two — one for me and one for Karen? I'll fuck off to New Zealand," he said.

"Who's Karen?" asked Miss X.

"Me girl."

"Your girl? Okay. I didn't know you had a girl."

"I'll get passports and stay over there and under a different name. I can stay over there, can't I? I don't have to apply to stay there do I?" Travers wanted to know. "If I was living over there, I'll start all over again. I'll get bail tomorrow. That'll be great and I'll just piss off. I've gotta find somewhere to hide. I don't know where I can hide."

"You can't. You can't afford to hide. You just gotta go. You just gotta get a boat and go," said Miss X.

"If I can get a passport."

"Listen to me. Passports (for New Zealand) didn't come out until 1982, right? Now if you go to New Zealand before then you don't need a passport. You just arrive there, not through one of the ports of entry. You just arrive anywhere on the coast and you can act as though you've been there for ages".

"Yeah, that's it. I'll do it. I wouldn't know where the fuck I was or anything . . ."

"You gotta go, you gotta go by plane or boat don't ya because you can't get there."

"By sea."

"You can't find it."

"I'm not gonna do it by meself. I'll take her, she'll come."

"Oh, yeah, when I leave I'll do everything I can to find Kerry."

"If I can get out on bail, which I hope, I might have a chance. If not I just gotta hide somewhere. You see, I've got nowhere I can go."

"I'll try, John. I'll try to hide you."

"It's just that I can't think of where."

Miss X then explained she would need a photo of him for a false passport and he said he would get one the next day. "Getting out of an international airport's gonna be real hard," she said.

"That's why I'll have to look a bit older."

"Getting you out would be easy as a seaman on a ship but getting Karen . . . Oh, she could just fly or even go on the ship. Stow away."

"I'll have to work it out."

"Haven't got much time. When you get out tomorrow you've gotta go then. You can't wait. We could always head straight up to North Queensland. We'll do everything, John, we've just gotta get you out, that's the hard part. I can't think apart from getting a fucking bulldozer through the wall. I can't think of any other way. A train through the wall, derail it. Well, it's a thought."

"I've got oxy there," he said, "but they'd see it. I've still got that fucking machine gun."

Travers told Miss X to go to a house in Granville to fetch "Gary and Mick . . . tell them to be in the (Blacktown) court with the shotties and a bit of back-up to blast me out."

Miss X said: "Derail the train and send it through the fucking walls."

Travers told Miss X if he got bail it would be "goodbye Australia". He said his girlfriend Karen would have to leave home.

"I didn't know she still lived at home. How old is she?"

"Sixteen."

"She's legal isn't she? All right then, so long as you trust her."

"Oh, yeah, I've never got on with a chick like I have with her."

"That's good. It's about time you got yourself a real nice lady."

Miss X promised Travers she would take a letter to his girlfriend for him. "Is there anything else you want me to say to her when I give it to her?"

"Just give it to her and say what, what I say and that from the bottom of me heart."

Travers then told Miss X why he killed Anita Cobby. She'd said, "John, because why? Why did you have to do that? Come here, come close, come close."

"Oh, yeah," he said. "We were all drunk and she's fucking seen all of us."

"What, she saw your faces?"

"Yeah and she got all our names cause I just . . ."

"She got your names!"

"Yeah."

"What, you were drunk and just talking among each other?"

"Yeah."

"Ooh!"

". . . and I just, fuck . . ."

"And you knew, you knew."

"Someone had to do it."

"And you knew, so what, the others said you had to do it?"

"Ah, they just, fuck, I said she's got to be done and they said . . ."

"Who said it had to be done? You?"

"All of us."

"You all agreed?"

"Yeah and they said, 'Go on Trawney, do your bit' so I just cut her."

"But that's not your thing, John. You haven't done that before have you?"

"No."

"And she'd seen you. And she saw your teardrop didn't she?"

"They weren't gonna do it so I had to."

"And the rotten bastards all fucked off on you."

"No-one wants to know me now."

"I do John, I still love you."

"Yeah, but I'm just saying they don't and I don't have to stay fucking cool though."

Miss X asked Travers why he hadn't tried to get rid of Anita Cobby's body. "Why did you leave the body there? Why didn't you piss it off? Get rid of it?"

"We were too scared to go back."

She realised then that the only remorse he felt was for himself . . . "That he was in the cell, that he was caged and he couldn't get out. That was the only remorse," she remembered.

While in the witness box, Miss X was surprised by Mick Murdoch's appearance. It was the best she had ever seen him look. Later she said, "I remember Mick wore glasses, a suit and he had his hair neat, combed and brushed back. He'd never worn it like that in his life. It wasn't him, he was portraying innocence.

"I truly feel that if it hadn't come out, Michael Murdoch would have gone to the police himself. He might have told Rose too. I doubt that he could live with this because he didn't have the strength to cope with it by himself."

When she stepped down from the witness box and was escorted out of the court through a door with green felt lining, Miss X breathed a sigh of relief. "It's over," she thought, "I can start living."

Chapter 31

Garry and Grace Lynch were composed throughout the trial. They sat with their friend Anne Farmer. They handled the ordeal well. Few things could have been harder to bear than having to listen to how their own child, their precious daughter, had died. The police, barristers and medical men spoke of Anita in court in clinical terms, as if she was just another statistic: the deceased, the victim, the corpse. They were not being disrespectful, it was just part of their job. And they talked about lacerations, contusions to the lateral aspect of the left thigh and uttered dozens of other complicated phrases. But to the Lynchs the deceased would always be Anita Lorraine Cobby, nee Lynch. She was their daughter, a vibrant, beautiful, decent woman who had suffered terribly and died violently. It was so unfair.

The police, in reality, didn't think of Anita as just another statistic. They did care about how she died. They cared too, about how her family would make it through the trial. They spoke with the Lynchs each morning before court. They talked with them again in the afternoon. Sometimes they had lunch with them. They didn't have to, but they wanted to. Their hearts went out to Grace and Garry Lycnh. Garry found the trial a terrible ordeal and sometimes skipped half a day. Once he took off to Lightning Ridge for a week's break.

During the 54 days of evidence the four accused spent their time listening on and off, but it was apparent that they often had difficulty understanding or following the proceedings. The legal arguments were complex and the jargon used frequently confusing. Gary Murphy had matters explained to him by his brother Michael, who sat next to him. When Les Murphy read something, his lips would silently form the words. And Murdoch doodled. He would scribble for hours on the back of a foolscap notepad. He was usually silent and he looked bored. Michael Murphy did take an interest in most of the proceedings and would often shake his head and grin at police during their evidence, indicating he didn't agree with it. The others only seemed to pay attention when their names were mentioned despite the fact that debate was often heated.

David Wetmore, representing Gary Murphy, was known as "Sandy". His long fair hair blended almost perfectly with his barrister's wig. Without that wig and his robes, he didn't look like a barrister, especially with the tiny diamond stud earring he wore. His broad Canadian accent would boom across the courtroom. He would subtly use his sense of humour to relieve the solemnity of the trial. Neck and neck in the good humour stakes was Michael Murphy's barrister Bill Hosking, a QC and a totally different style of man to Sandy Wetmore. Hosking, always in a dark suit, would take to addressing the jury or a witness with his hands clasped in front of him in a choir boy grip. He had a round face, pale skin and could recite apt pieces of Shakespeare at any given time, always to the blank stares of the defendants. He knew his law and pushed it to the limit.

Marcus Bleasel, representing Michael Murdoch, was a tall, thin man with a neat beard with reddish highlights through it. In his 30s, he was younger than the other barristers around the bar table. Bradley Mulligan, Leslie Murphy's counsel, was a personable-looking fellow. He was quiet and sometimes had a red complexion. He would often start a phrase or question and then say, "I'll withdraw that."

Justice Maxwell was regarded as firm and fair. He had a wonderful ear for detail and could recount sections of evidence to counsel, sometimes weeks later. He tolerated no nonsense in his court but he sometimes grinned, quickly, at the antics around the bar table. Usually these revolved around how far counsel could twist "my *learn*ed friend's" evidence to suit their own advantage. But not much went on in Justice Maxwell's courtroom that he didn't know about. One of the court police officers, Richard Hoodcamp, was an amateur cartoonist. He escorted the prisoners from gaol to court and back again each day and, to while away the hours in between, he would satirise the key issues or light moments in evidence. The cartoonist would quietly sketch away, hidden, he thought, from view, behind an old wooden bench to one side of the courtroom. At the end of the trial, Justice Maxwell discreetly requested copies of all 33 of his works. Unbeknown to His Honour, court officials, police, journalists and lawyers made the same request.

In the middle of the police grilling, there were a few light moments to savour. One came when after nearly two days in the witness box, a police officer became tired of watching the four accused smirk, laugh and shake their heads at him every time he answered a question. In the absence of the jury, while counsel were debating a legal point and most eyes were elsewhere, the officer faced the defendants, grabbed his tie and pulled it up around his neck, as in a hangman's noose. It was over in a second. No-one saw it, except a handful of media, one police colleague and two of the accused. The looks on the faces of the two defendants were priceless.

Another light moment came from Speed Kennedy. His reply in evidence to a question brought muffled laughter and even raised a faint smile on His Honour's face. When asked by Bill Hosking, for Michael Murphy, why the defendant had a carpet burn or graze on his face after his arrest, the burly Kennedy replied, "It may have been because I had my foot on his head as he lay on the floor." He was explaining how he had to take this action to retrieve his handcuffs.

The 20-minute morning teabreak was always welcome. Most mornings the media would dash down to a French patisserie a block away for a coffee and a sausage roll. The next break came at 1pm and many lunch hours were spent eating $3 hot club-style meals at the Grosvenor Club.

The Lynchs would park their car there. The manager, after recognising Garry Lynch during one of his lunchtime visits, offered him a reserved parking spot in the club car park. It was a fine gesture because parking around the court was scarce and anyone managing to fluke a spot would be forever running out to feed the meter. It was often easier to risk a $25 parking fine and take your chances on the parking police passing you by.

Inside the court, the evidence made compelling listening. The police were given a torrid time by defence lawyers. Their reputations were questioned, their values were queried and their professionalism doubted. They were accused of fabricating the defendants' statements, of brutality and making up evidence. Often it seemed as if the police were on trial, too.

Travers was the only one who didn't dispute his record of interview, but he could hardly have denied making it. After all, his confession was on tape. Travers, alone, didn't allege he'd been set-up, beaten or verballed by police.

One friend of the Lynch family remarked during the trial, "They (the accused) complain about all the things they say police did to them but think what *they* did to Anita. I wonder if they have thought for even one minute if *she* was scared or hurting."

Defence counsel gave Maxine Greensmith a testing time after she admitted she had changed some of her evidence because she was frightened. Mrs Greensmith agreed at the committal proceedings she had omitted to say she had seen Gary Murphy standing around the fire in the Travers' backyard on the night of the murder. She stood by her claim that she had seen the back and side of a man's face and recognised him by these features. This was crucial to Murphy's not guilty plea.

The issues were sometimes complex and confusing. For many hours, sometimes days, legal debate and evidence was heard in the absence of the jury, until it could be decided whether it was too prejudicial to the defendants for the jury to be exposed to it.

The jury was granted a request to visit the scene of the murder, so they could get their bearings and have a clearer definition of some of the evidence. A small airport bus was used to take the group, accompanied by court officials, to Reen Rd. The media was ordered by Justice Maxwell not to approach any juror and not to publish or screen any photos or film of the group, unless at a distance, in order to protect their identity. As the jurors were taken into the paddock the media waited along the roadway about 30 metres away while their news helicopters hovered overhead recording the event from the air. The spot where Anita's body was discovered was marked by a bright yellow witch hat.

In the police statements tendered to the court, Murdoch and the three Murphys each denied having sexual intercourse with their victim. But all five men alleged the other four had sex with her. Gary Murphy claimed he tried to have oral sex but couldn't. Murdoch and the three Murphys nominated Travers as the one who had killed

Anita Cobby and, in a statement tendered to the court by Sgt Rosetta, Travers, when asked after his arrest who had killed Mrs Cobby, replied, "I did."

An article in *The Sydney Morning Herald* by the paper's court reporter Jenny Cooke probably gives the best insight into the tendering process for the accused's records of interview during the trial. Upon acceptance as an exhibit, each interview had to be read to the jury. The job fell to Justice Maxwell's associate Beverley Dalley. Jenny Cooke wrote, "From the prosecution point of view she was probably the best person to read them. Ms Dalley is a thin, almost skinny woman in her early 40s. She looks like an 18th century governess. She is obviously a nice person. And she wasn't looking forward to this trial. Every time the alleged admissions were read out — and they took at least 20 minutes each time — most people in the court actively hated those four men. The quotes were horrific, full of swear words and phrases about sex that debased this God-given act to the runtings of an animal. Miss Dalley would pause, take a gulp and look towards the jury as if to assure them she didn't normally use words like 'f . . .' and 'c . . .' or phrases such as 'couldn't get a fat'." In fact, hearing these expletives uttered by Justice Maxwell and other legal counsel was unsettling, to say the least.

Chapter 32

The series of events culminating in and immediately following Anita Cobby's death are best portrayed in the five accused's own words, their records of interview. In the hours after their arrests each man gave police similar versions of what happened on the night of February 2, 1986. Each version roughly corresponds, despite the denials later by the three Murphys and Murdoch that the contents of their interviews were not what they had told police. The men said in court the interviews presented by police were fabricated and their signatures at the bottom of each of the pages had only been secured under duress. The threats and beatings by police during their interrogation, they said, had terrified them into signing the interviews.

Only John Travers, whose story is distinctly similar to the other four, didn't dispute the contents of his record of interview. Instead he admitted guilt and pleaded guilty.

When these records of interview were read to the court, their frankness shocked listeners. The men's descriptions of what happened during the hour or more they spent with Anita Cobby are graphically brutal. The language is foul. Each spoke about the atrocities committed as if they were everyday occurrences. Each man minimised his own participation in the abuse of Anita Cobby and each tried to distance himself from the act of the killing, blaming John Travers alone for the death of the nurse.

Each also has a different recollection about how they came together that night. Gary Murphy said that on the afternoon of February 2, he and his brother Mick were working on his car at Ray and Judy Paterson's home in Tivoli Place at Doonside. Murphy said he had three cans of beer and his brother five cans, before they left around 6.30pm to go to the Travers' home.

Les Murphy was at Travers' house with his girlfriend Lisa and

Murdoch. Gary Murphy told how plans were being made with another unidentified man to steal a tractor, although Les Murphy was under the impression they were going to steal a car.

Michael Murphy's recollections though, were that all the men had been at the Doonside Hotel drinking for a couple of hours when Travers wanted to go to see a mate at Windsor. "Les was complaining about his car having no brakes so we went and picked up the HT," Michael Murphy said. The five men left in the 1970 HT Holden Premier sedan that Travers told police he had stolen from a Seven Hills home the previous Tuesday. He had hot-wired it to get it going, placing a screw driver on the starter motor and wrapping some silver cigarette foil around the fuses after he blew them all trying to start it the first time. When the vehicle was stolen Travers explained it was green but it was sprayed undercoat grey a few days later and the number plates had been changed. The plates, Michael Murphy revealed, were from an HT Holden that belonged to his brother Bernie Murphy. That car had been written off in an accident and the plates had been kept. The reason the car was resprayed according to Gary Murphy, was because "Mick Murphy wanted to keep it".

Travers admitted on the night Anita Cobby was killed he, the Murphy brothers and Murdoch went for a drive. "I was on the turps and I was pretty blind . . . I remember mainly going out for a drive in the car, we were looking for something to steal to make some money . . ." Travers said.

According to Michael Murphy, when they arrived at Windsor, they pulled up outside a house and, "Travers went inside and was in there for about 10 minutes and when he came out he jumped in the car and (we) started driving back to his place."

There's confusion about who drove the car. Gary and Michael Murphy both say Michael Murphy was driving when Anita was picked up but they changed spots shortly after. Travers was giving directions but "I didn't know where to drive so I told Gary to drive . . . we swapped places as the car was still going," Michael Murphy told police. Les Murphy, though, recalled Travers driving, with Murdoch sitting in the front and the three brothers in the back. He said they were "talking about what kind of car we wanted (to steal). We were in Newton Rd, near a roundabout. Mick Murphy and John

Travers saw a girl and pointed her out to us. We needed money for petrol. We was just going to grab her handbag until John said, 'Let's take her with us.' We got around the corner, changed drivers, Gary and John changed places of driving, so John sat in the back and Gary was driving. Gary did a U-turn . . . we drove up the road to the girl . . ."

Travers told police the car pulled up in front of Anita. "I opened the back door, jumped out and tried to drag her in but couldn't get her in and Mick (Murdoch) jumped out and grabbed the other half and we got her in the car." As the car door slammed shut, with Anita Cobby struggling inside, John Travers remembers turning around to see "a bloke run up from behind as we were taking off". Stephen Hodson reached the footpath as the car drove away up the road. Travers kept staring at Hodson until the car went through the intersection a short distance away.

When Det Sgt Kennedy asked Michael Murphy, "Was there any reason why she was selected?" Murphy replied, "John just saw her and wanted her." He recalled hearing Anita scream once when she was being dragged into the car. Once inside, she was thrown across the men in the back seat's laps and Michael Murphy said, "John and Mick started ripping her clothes off as soon as she got into the car." The pair ordered Anita to take her clothes off several times and she refused, telling them, "Leave me alone, I'm married". Travers retorted, "Well, you've had it before".

Les Murphy said he saw Travers and Michael Murphy "just slapping her around. One of them put his hand over her mouth" and Michael Murphy said Travers punched Anita in the back of the head about three times and told her to shut up. He also told police Les leaned over from the front seat and punched her hard in the head.

The stolen HT Holden sped from the abduction scene in Newton Rd and headed towards the Great Western Highway a few kilometres away. At one point, according to Michael Murphy, the car stalled and the men believed they were out of petrol. They managed to get it going again and drove towards the nearest petrol station on the busy Great Western Highway, across the road from the Prospect Hotel. Murdoch said Anita ". . . was screaming, kicking and fighting." He was rummaging through Anita's bag looking for money as they pulled up beside the petrol bowser closest to the roadway and furthest from the cashier's office. Now their weeping hostage was naked. Travers had pulled her jeans off and Michael Murphy removed her top. Travers asked Murdoch to give him a knife he'd stashed in the car but when he couldn't find it, Travers leaned over, felt around the car's console and retrieved it himself. "Here it is," Michael Murphy remembered Travers saying as he held it in his hand. "Don't show her the knife," Gary Murphy yelled, but it was too late. Travers was tapping the knife on Anita's back as she was crouched on the floor of the car, telling her not to scream and not to say anything. "Don't scream and you won't get hurt," Travers threatened.

When asked by police who paid for the petrol, Murdoch replied, "She did." He said Les Murphy took "20-something dollars out of her purse." And it was Les Murphy who was given the job of filling the car. He claimed it cost only $10. "I think that's about all she had," he said. Michael Murphy believed the petrol cost $15.

The men drove out of the petrol station with their captive still on the floor in the back of the car. Travers suggested they take her to near the Blacktown Drive-in, nearby. He hadn't been to that area before "but I knew there was a bit of bush there". Travers gave the directions to do a U-turn across the busy six-lane highway. "We were driving back along the highway and John said, 'turn left'," Michael Murphy said. "We drove up this dark road . . ."

Murdoch recalled Travers "put (Anita) on her knees in the back seat" and raped her. "Then Mick had a turn . . ." While Anita was being raped, Murdoch said, "I was sittin' in the front going through her bag with Les." It was then when Murdoch recalls one of the men saying Anita was menstruating.

In the dark the men drove the stolen car down Reen Rd. It was quiet and there was no street lighting but the moon's radiance was bright enough for Mick Murdoch to see a man on his front lawn near the end of the road, where it turned into a dead-end. But John Reen took no notice. There were always cars driving down his road night and day, looking for a quiet spot. Mostly it was couples looking for a place to make love. So John Reen usually ignored them because they were gone within a few hours.

The stolen Holden pulled up and did a U-turn, parking on the side of the road, about halfway down. The men took Anita out of the car and Les Murphy said he punched her once in the shoulder before she was laid down beside the barbed-wire fence, on the grass. "I think she was unconscious because she had been punched around a bit," Les Murphy said. "John Travers laid on top of the girl . . . and he had sex with her."

It was then when Les spotted a car parked a little further down the road. "... Les kept going on about the car being down in front . . . I was standing near the back door of the car telling Les to shut his mouth," Michael Murphy said. Mick Murdoch suggested they all move down into the paddock. He claimed it was Gary Murphy who had sex with Anita beside the fence and then Les Murphy followed while at the same time Gary Murphy forced his victim to have oral sex with him. Murdoch remembered that Travers went back to the car to retrieve his knife and Les Murphy said he saw Travers tuck the knife in the back of his trousers.

Again there is confusion about how Anita was taken into the paddock. John Travers thought she was carried in while Les Murphy said, "We threw her over the barbed-wire fence, I had hold of one of her arms." Michael Murphy claims he lifted up the wire so Anita could climb through. He said Travers was pushing her and Murdoch grabbed Anita's hair and warned her, "Keep your head down, don't look at anyone." Murdoch initially told police, "They put her over the fence" but then changed his mind saying, "No, I'll tell you proper. I jumped over the fence first, they put her through the fence, Mick (Murphy) had his arm around her chest and he was walking her down the paddock." He said Anita "screamed a little bit" when she was being taken into the paddock. Les Murphy said Anita "was staggering and I had hold of her arm" as they walked.

Michael Murphy, however, had a different view. He said he watched Travers and Murdoch put Anita through the fence while Les Murphy ". . . was saying something to her and he kept trying to grab hold of her." Murphy thought his brother was trying to rape Anita and he told him to leave her alone. "He got the shits and grabbed hold of her arm. Him, Mick and John walked her down the paddock." At this time Gary Murphy claims he and his brother Michael were sitting in the car and watched as the men walked Anita down the paddock. "Someone had hold of her . . . he had his arm around her." Then they caught up with the others.

When the group had steered Anita Cobby through the knee-high grass to a spot between two slender gums, Travers claimed he moved a few feet away from the others. "I was just laying down getting head spins." He said he didn't have sex with Anita a second time.

Then, according to Michael Murdoch, Michael Murphy raped Anita and then forced her to have oral sex with him. He said that Les Murphy attempted to have anal sex with the woman . . . "And then they were all finished with her."

Murdoch was asked by Ian Kennedy, "Did you have intercourse with her?" "No," Murdoch answered. "Why not?" "Because I didn't want to." "Any reason why?" "Because I don't get into rape."

However Gary Murphy claimed Murdoch did have intercourse with Anita Cobby twice after she was taken into the paddock. He claimed Les Murphy raped her first and that he was followed by Michael Murphy, Murdoch, Travers, then he thought, Murdoch again. He admitted inserting his penis in his victim's mouth "for about 10 minutes". Gary Murphy told police Murdoch and possibly Travers also had oral sex with Anita. When asked what condition Anita was in, he answered, "She wasn't too happy about things, but she wasn't crying then."

Michael Murphy claimed his brother Les and Murdoch argued over who would rape their victim first. He said he had tried to have oral sex with her but he could not get an erection. Gary Murphy and Murdoch, he claimed, had tried to insert their penises in the woman's mouth. Michael Murphy said Travers either tried to, or did rape the victim again. When asked what he was doing when all this was going on, Michael Murphy replied, "Just standing there . . . I just gave up."

Les Murphy, too, claimed he could not get an erection. He said Michael Murphy "went berserk" on Anita, raping and assaulting her. While she was conscious all of the men, he said, repeatedly threatened to rape their victim. Murphy told police Anita kept begging them, "Let me go." He said just as his brother was about to rape Anita a car came down the road with its headlights on. The light startled the men and they all ran through the long grass heading back towards the highway to hide, except Travers. Les Murphy told police, "John Travers lay down beside the girl amongst the grass." Michael Murphy said he heard Travers call out, "Come back."

Again, the men have different versions of what happened next.

Les Murphy told police they all returned to where Anita was ". . . she was still unconscious. I was going to lay on her to have intercourse with her. Mick Murphy said, 'No, let's go.' He whispered something to John Travers. I don't know what they whispered. Gary, Mick Murdoch and myself were going to the car. Mick (Murphy) was coming with us but he turned back. Gary, myself and Mick Murdoch were at the car, John Travers and Mick Murphy started to run up to us from where the girl was lying . . . one of them said to us 'Get into the car and let's go.'" He said the last time he saw Anita Cobby "she was dazed but she was breathing".

Gary Murphy said he did hear what his brother Michael said to Travers before Travers went back to where Anita Cobby was lying. "John come over towards Mick Murphy and all I heard was, Mick Murphy said, 'Do your own thing.'" Gary Murphy said the four then ran to the car, leaving Travers in the paddock with Anita Cobby. The last time Gary Murphy saw Anita Cobby she was lying on her side, crying.

The group didn't return to their victim after running from the glare of the headlights, according to Michael Murphy, but he saw John Travers trying to drag her by the arm. "She looked to be unconscious, and John said, 'I'm gunna cut her throat.' I said, 'No, come on, leave her.' John said, 'No, she's seen us.' I said, 'No, come on, leave her, she had her head down, leave her.' . . . the four of us started walking up the paddock and John went back to her."

Murdoch believed Anita Cobby was unconscious at this stage because he'd seen "Les kick her in the head". Murdoch said he heard Travers say he was going to cut their victim's throat because "She's recognised the whole lot of us." Murdoch claimed he and the Murphy brothers walked towards the car. Les Murphy heard Travers and his brother Michael whispering then Travers said, "She's got to go 'cause she knows our names."

Travers claims Anita was unconscious when he went back to the limp form with the intention of cutting her throat. ". . . we were worried that she'd identify us, so we agreed to get rid of her . . . they were saying 'What will we do if she identifies us?' and then I heard

'Trawney, do your thing.' . . . I thought they meant get rid of her." Murdoch said ". . . he was sitting on her back, had her hair pulled back and I just turned around and went."

Travers thought he cut Anita Cobby's throat twice. When asked by Det Sgt Rosetta did he recall seeing any blood, Travers replied that he had, on his hands, on the knife, on his feet and jeans. Travers said he thought one or two of the others were standing near him when he cut Anita's throat but he could not remember which ones.

The men were at the car when Travers ran back to them nearly a minute later. He jumped in and said, "Quick, go." Michael Murphy told police, "John come running up with blood all over him. He said, 'I cut her throat.' I think he said, 'I cut a couple of fingers off 'cause she put her hand up.' He was big-noting about how she put her hand up. He said, 'It's me first one.'" Murdoch asked him what it felt like. Travers mindlessly answered, "Like nothing." Murdoch said when Travers told them what he had done he seemed to be in a "quiet" mood.

Gary Murphy drove the others away in the Holden, leaving Anita Cobby bleeding to death in the paddock. By the time they had reached the turn-off to the highway, she was gone.

It wasn't until they reached the Great Western Highway that Gary Murphy said Travers "told us what he'd done . . . he said, 'I killed her, I cut her throat.'" Murphy saw the blood on Travers' hands and clothes and noticed his knife.

Gary Murphy drove them to Ray Paterson's house, according to Les Murphy, and "We stayed there for about five minutes, wondering what we were going to do," he said. Travers said he wanted to go back to his place to have a shower and change his clothes. Gary Murphy told Travers, "You shouldn't have cut her throat." Mick Murdoch laughed and said Travers was mad.

Travers went inside while the others went to the caravan at the back of the house. On the way through, Travers noticed his mother in the loungeroom. Lisa Travers was in the kitchen of the caravan when "Someone commented on the blood that was on John in front of Lisa," Michael Murphy said. "Murdoch said there was a dog barking at us so he cut it up. Lisa got the shits and walked back inside."

While Travers was in the shower washing his clothes, Murdoch gathered up Anita Cobby's belongings, poured lawn mower petrol over them and started a fire on the cement slab in the backyard. He'd worked out that if anyone asked why he was lighting a fire so late at night he would tell them he was burning rubbish. He threw everything on the fire. Her dark cloth bag with designs on it, her purse, a lunchbox, a pair of sunglasses and her makeup bag were all destroyed. Every trace of Anita Cobby's belongings were gone. Except her shoes, which Murdoch said Gary Murphy asked for.

Michael Murphy thought he and Gary had left during the burning of the clothes. Les Murphy was watching TV when his brothers came in and told him they were going home. Gary Murphy said he borrowed Les' station waggon and took Michael Murphy with him.

When he came out of the shower, Travers didn't see his mother but he said the four men were sitting at the kitchen table. Les remembered Travers talking about what had happened that night with him and Murdoch. ". . . (Travers) showed us the knife. He told us how he killed her by pulling her head up with her hair and slit her throat," he said. Travers claimed after he had cleaned up the men all "went for a drive out Windsor . . . then I come home and went to bed . . . Mick (Murdoch) went to bed, he lives there too, and Les went out the back to the caravan, I don't know about the other two," he said.

Michael Murphy told police that none of them had returned to the paddock to see if the girl was dead. "I didn't want her to be killed. He (Travers) is a maniac. It's his fault. I told him not to kill her." Murdoch said at some stage at the Travers' home there was a discussion about burying the body "but we didn't want to go back there," he said. The day after the killing Michael Murphy said Travers came around to see him about moving the body but he had told him, "I'm not going near it."

Days later, Travers claimed, the ashes from the fire were taken to the nearby Richmond Rd tip along with a trailer full of rubbish by him, his brother Peter, Mick Murdoch and Les Murphy.

According to Les Murphy, the car used to drive Anita Cobby to her death was used by his brothers after the murder. "Mick and Gary were driving around in it for a while, (they) came over to our place and told us they had to get rid of the car. They asked me to help them and I said, 'Yes'. I had a fight with Mick, walked home and I heard they went and dumped the car.

About five days after Anita Cobby died the HT Holden was dumped then destroyed. Michael Murphy told police they had to "get rid of the evidence . . . our prints. There would have been blood from John." He drove the vehicle to a street not far from Travers' place but he couldn't remember the exact location. "As I jumped out I went to rip the back plate off but Mick and John had thrown petrol all over it . . . the car was up in flames so we couldn't go back." Travers said he threw a match onto it and the last time he saw the car it was "burnt out".

A Blacktown Council employee found the wreck with one number plate on the rear a few blocks from the Travers home. He photographed it and confirmed it didn't match the number plate that was on it and was in fact a stolen, green HT Holden from Seven Hills. As a matter of course the council handed over the photograph to police but by the time police went to check it, the wreck had disappeared. At that stage police had no idea how close they were to capturing Anita Cobby's killers.

During their periods of interrogation, none of the men had contact with each other so there could have been no collusion concerning their versions of events. Indeed, after completing his interview, Michael Murphy was handed a carbon copy of Murdoch's interview to read. He heatedly contradicted Murdoch's version, complaining that Murdoch was claiming he did not have sex with Anita Cobby when, according to Murphy, it was Gary Murphy who did not. Then, after reading a photostat copy of his brother Les' interview, Murphy told police, "He's a liar. He's trying to place the blame on everybody else." He then read his own and was able to correct a mistake he said had been made in his. He said the interview had him attempting to rape Anita Cobby beside the fence. That part, he said, was right, but the section describing him trying to force oral sex on his victim beside the fence was wrong. "I didn't try to do that until we got into the paddock," he said.

Police were still accused in court of fabricating the records of interviews.

Chapter 33

After being charged in Blacktown court for the murder of Anita, Gary Murphy was escorted to Westmead Hospital, where he was treated for his facial injuries. X-rays showed he had a broken jaw and grazes, caked with trickles of dried blood, were clearly visible on his cheeks. Police maintained Murphy had been injured the previous week in a brawl outside the Blacktown RSL but Murphy insisted he was hurt during his arrest. Official police photographs of Gary and Michael Murphy, taken after their arrests, ironically were missing. Defence counsel claimed the photos would have clearly shown the injuries and aided them in the men's defence of police brutality. The NSW Ombudsman's office launched an inquiry into the missing rolls of film and tracked them down to the police scientific branch where they were sent to be developed. The film was lost after arriving but the report concluded there was nothing sinister in the disappearance. If necessary, defence counsel could have subpeonaed media photographs showing close-ups of the same injuries.

Sandy Wetmore alleged to the court his client Gary Murphy had been subjected to violence during the arrest and hadn't been tackled at all by police. This was denied by all police involved in the arrest. TRG Sen Const Ian Donaldson told the court that during the raid on the townhouse at Tari Way he had seen Gary Murphy at the rear of the premises, moving away from house. "I called out, 'Stop, police!' and then put my shotgun on the ground and chased him 20 metres and tackled him from behind." The impact, he said, caused Murphy to collide face first with the fence. He was then assisted by two other TRG officers, Sgt Moule and Const Duncan. The three subdued Murphy, the court heard, and then handed him over to Const Paul Davies and Blacktown's Const Milton Legge, who had been searching underneath the townhouse. The pair walked Murphy to a waiting police car.

The defence argued Murphy could not have sustained the facial injuries in the way police said he had. In fact, neighbours of the women who lived in the Tari Way townhouse where the Murphys were arrested had talked to a Channel 7 news journalist the morning after the raid. They told how they were scared after seeing men with guns lurking in the yard. Some of the neighbours said they were unaware a raid was going on and had gone outside to watch the helicopter that hovered overhead. One neighbour said, "The ungodly screams out of that boy (Gary Murphy). I'll never forget them as long as I live . . . He just got laid into. When he stumbled, he never hurt himself, he was down on the ground." One neighbour had looked over the fence into the yard. "They hit him with the butt of a gun first of all. Then they booted him . . . they weren't nice to him at all . . . they had him on the ground, they had a foot on his back and he never fought back . . . they dragged him up the path, they didn't walk him up the path, they threw him against the tree . . . he was thrown down onto the ground. The police had their feet on him again and they laid into him. We're not saying he's innocent, we're not saying he's guilty, but you're supposed to be innocent until *proven* guilty. Three against one . . . no one needed to do that."

Just over three weeks before the end of the trial, defence counsel for Gary Murphy notified the court he would be claiming an alibi. This came as a surprise. No mention had previously been made in court of an alibi. On Wednesday, May 13, Gary Murphy made an unsworn statement from the dock. As the evidence was unsworn he couldn't be cross-examined before the jury. He said he had not even been at the scene of the crime. Murphy claimed on the night of the murder he was at the Doonside Hotel with his brother Mick, John Travers and Ray Paterson. "We had been drinking all day. Mick and John Travers left the hotel together and me and Ray stayed there until closing time. Me and Ray Paterson left together. I don't know where we went. I can't remember. It wasn't important at the time but I do know I was not at a rape or a murder. That's one thing I would remember."

Murphy told the court he first knew he was wanted for murder when a friend told him the police were looking for him. "Then another friend told me that the police were going to shoot me on sight and I was even more scared. I was scared I was going to be shot." He said back at the police station after his arrest a detective threw some papers on a table and told him to start signing them. He grabbed me by the head, by the top of the hair and kept jerking me back. I just grabbed the pen to start signing papers, sign anything that was put in front of me just to let the police leave me alone." He said he also signed another piece of paper so "there would be no more hitting". Later, after he was taken to Parklea Gaol, he said, a prison doctor examined him and found he had a broken jaw that needed to be wired for several weeks. Gary Murphy closed his address by saying, "I did not rape, I did not murder, I was not there."

Murphy still claims he didn't leave the hotel with Travers on the night of the murder. "I left with Ray Paterson and we went home," he said recently.

Even now, Les Murphy says his brother Gary wasn't with them on the night. When asked was his brother Gary there, he shook his head and answered, "No." But each of the men had the opportunity to make the claim when in court. Why had they not? Perhaps significantly, Les Murphy made no mention of Gary's being absent as recently as July, 1990, when he was back in Darlinghurst Supreme Court for a re-trial.

* * *

Les Murphy told the court he was attacked by police during his arrest at the Markham home at Granville in the early hours of February 24. Police say they found him huddling under a blanket between two women, one of them pregnant, on a mattress in a bedroom of the home. According to police he was pulled out of bed, forced onto the floor face down and handcuffed. Murphy said he was struck across the head with a torch by one of the officers before being led to the car. The allegations were denied by all four arresting police, Sgt O'Toole, Sgt Waters, Const Heskett and Const Davies.

Murphy said he was denied the chance to call his solicitor. He said police took his address book from him at the house and despite requests for it to be returned so he could call his solicitor, he was ignored. Les Murphy also claimed he signed the record of interview attributed to him because he was scared of the police after being threatened and beaten.

During Les Murphy's unchallenged 18-minute speech from the dock he said he wanted to give "my side of the story — what really happened". Dressed in a tie, grey shirt and grey woollen vest, Murphy started, "I'm not very good at giving speeches" and then told how he had known Travers through his girlfriend Lisa, Travers' sister, with whom he had been going out for a month. He said he only went out on the night of February 2 because he had been drinking. He said he'd been in the front seat of the car, "really off my face", when Travers pulled a screaming girl into the car. He said there had been no prior discussion about pulling her into the car. "I heard a woman scream. She was pulled in the car by John Travers. I did not hit her in the car. I did not know her. I did not have sex with the girl beside the car or anywhere near Reen Rd. I remember seeing John Travers taking the girl into the paddock. When he came back to the car he was covered in blood. I did not know John Travers had killed Mrs Cobby."

He told the court he hid from police because he did not think he would "have a fair go" from them because of what he had seen and heard through the media. He claimed he had been struck on the head with a torch and called a "fucking liar" when he was arrested and then on the way to Blacktown after the arrest he had been "smacked in the mouth" by a police officer and told he would be taken to a back street and "fixed up". "I got really scared and didn't know what was going to happen." At the station he had received several "smacks in the mouth" from police and was called a "fucking liar" and was warned to tell the truth. He told the jury he didn't reply but was "really scared and didn't want to get hit anymore".

Murphy claimed Det Raue had escorted him to the toilet and given him a handkerchief to wipe some dried blood from a cut on his forehead. He alleged many of the questions in the record of interview were not even put to him nor did he give some of the answers recorded. "The reason I signed the record of interview (was) because I was scared, scared of Det Raue and the way I was being treated by police, kicked, punched and slapped around, and the threats I had on the way up to the police station. I signed the record of interview because I wanted to get out of that room. I would like to say I didn't know John Travers had killed the girl. I had a girlfriend at the time and I was happy with her. I didn't know he (Travers) would do that. I wanted to tell the police everything I knew but I just didn't trust them because of what the papers said and everyone else said. I was afraid of what the police might do to me. I am telling the truth. I ask you to believe me. So help me God. Thank you."

Murphy sat down and put his head in his hands and then wiped his eyes when tears briefly filled them. He was shaking and kept wiping his eyes with a handkerchief until his solicitor Marcus Solomon walked to the front of the dock to see if he was alright. Murphy's speech had been punctuated by long pauses and the way it was spoken sounded like he had carefully memorised it. Justice Maxwell reminded the jury the statement was not made under oath and to disregard Murphy's words "So help me God" at the end of the speech.

During cross examination Det Raue denied Murphy had been slapped and abused by detectives or that he had offered him a handkerchief. He said he saw no marks on his forehead and no blood from any wounds. Raue also denied he had been made a sergeant directly as a result of his work on the case. In fact, Raue had sat for and passed his sergeants exam before the Cobby investigation. But the normal waiting period had to elapse before the appointment took effect. The promotion was duly made and Det Kevin Raue gave evidence as Det Sgt Raue.

Det Heskett denied an accusation that he had struck Les Murphy with a torch during his arrest at Granville. Heskett admitted he did have a police issue torch in his possession that night but it was not used to strike Murphy on the forehead. Bradley Mulligan also claimed Heskett's notebook entry, relating to a conversation where Murphy admitted his involvement in the murder, was fabricated because it wasn't signed by Murphy.

Heskett said that during the nine-page record of interview Les Murphy "had no problems whatsoever" understanding questions put to him and he had voluntarily indicated various things when he went on the run-around with police on the morning of his arrest.

* * *

Michael Murphy claimed that his record of interview was secured by a series of assaults by detectives who came into the interview room during the morning and bashed him.

Addressing the jury, Michael Murphy said, "It was a terrible thing that John Travers done to Mrs Cobby (he consistently pronounced her name 'Cobey'). He must have been insane . . ."

He said that for most of February 2, the day Anita disappeared, he and his brother Gary had been drinking beer and smoking pot as they worked on Gary's car at Doonside. "We started at 10.30am and between us we drank a whole carton of stubbies and had half a deal of marijuana." Then he said between 5pm and 8pm he had been drinking with Travers, whom he'd known only slightly for two weeks, at the Doonside Hotel and after Travers had driven them to a mate's place at Windsor Michael Murphy said he rolled eight marijuana joints. They smoked three, which made him "stoned". On the way back from Windsor, he told the jury, he was driving when Travers called out very quickly to "stop here" which he did and Travers dragged a girl he hadn't seen before inside. "I sung out, 'Leave her alone' but by that time it was too late. He said he was nervous, didn't know what was happening and told of Travers taking Mrs Cobby into the paddock for a short time. "I didn't want to have nothing to do with what was going on . . . at no time in or out of the car did I punch Anita Cobby." After Travers admitted cutting Anita's throat on the drive from Reen Rd back to Doonside, Michael Murphy said he had abused Travers who then just "walked inside". "I should have went to the police earlier. I don't know why I didn't."

Michael Murphy also made allegations of mistreatment by police and said he had nearly passed out after being hit in the back of the head with what he thought was a shotgun during his arrest at Glenfield. He said while being bashed and kicked by police his head had been pushed into a lounge pillow. He said that later at the station he was handcuffed to a chair while being interviewed and had been bashed twice by groups of detectives. He said he had told them he refused to say anything unless his solicitor was present but eventually signed the record of interview because "I was tired, I was frightened and I was scared".

He claimed he told a senior officer at the time the interview was involuntary "but he took no notice of me . . . them answers in the record of interview are definitely not mine". "At no time did I touch Mrs Cobby at all. I know it's a terrible thing what happened to Mrs Cobby but I am not guilty of this crime. Thank you."

Near the end of the trial Murphy leapt to his feet and cried, "I've had enough . . . I'm not guilty, I'm just not guilty! It's giving me the shits!" Bill Hosking calmed him down.

* * *

In Michael Murdoch's unsworn statement from the dock he claimed, "I never laid a hand on Mrs Cobby." Referring to notes, Murdoch said he was "very sorry about what happened . . . I am guilty of stealing a motor vehicle but I didn't want her to be abducted and I didn't want her to be raped and I certainly didn't want her to be murdered." He said he was unemployed in January and February of that year, ". . . I left school early because I was not very good at reading or writing."

Murdoch said he was questioned by police and gave a record of interview before being charged with murder. He didn't recall giving several of the answers contained in the interview and didn't remember hearing some of the questions. Murdoch admitted taking "three Serapax tablets" on the night he was interviewed and recalled he was very tired during the questions. He said Sgt Rosetta threatened him and said he would "smash a baseball bat and stick it up your arse . . ."

In Murdoch's version of events the jury heard he went with John Travers to a friend's brother's house where "we were drinking beer and smoking marijuana" for about 15 minutes. He, Travers, Les Murphy and Mick Murphy were driving around Blacktown when they saw a woman. "John said, 'Pull over and I'll grab her handbag.'" Travers had pulled her in and "me and Les went through her handbag looking for money for petrol". He said at "no time was there any discussion about rape, let alone murdering her".

He claimed Travers told Mick Murphy to drive around to Reen Rd and on the way Travers was raping Mrs Cobby in the back seat of the car. "I didn't have sex with her in any way. I was terrified by what was going on and there appeared nothing I could do to help Mrs Cobby." After Anita was taken into the paddock, "he (John Travers) came running up to the car and we took off. It really spun me out at the time". Murdoch thanked the jury for listening and sat down.

Chapter 34

In his final address to the jury, Alan Saunders was scathing in his attack on the four defendants and the explanations they gave for their involvement in the murder. He said Anita Cobby suffered "two hours of terror, torture and degradation" at the hands of "craven cowards in an orgy of lust". Saunders said she had suffered systematic beatings by the men in a most savage and brutal attack . . . that the sex acts had been committed "in a most unbelievably callous fashion".

Anita Cobby, he said, had been "the victim of unbridled lust culminating in the most brutal murder this state had ever known". Saunders said after Mrs Cobby had been killed the men went "straight away to Tich Place, Doonside, and burnt her clothing. They then burnt the car as well because it had fingerprints on it. What an indication of guilt that is."

The jury retired to consider its verdict before the lunchbreak. During the nine hours they deliberated, they asked for several sections of the evidence to be read again to them. A particular point of concern was whether any of the accused were intoxicated at the time of the murder by alcohol or drugs, therefore reducing their culpability.

Just after 7pm, more than 50 people — media and members of the public, were evacuated from the Darlinghurst court complex and the floodlit court compound after an anonymous telephone call to the Sydney Police Centre threatened a bomb would explode at the court. The male caller said a hand grenade would be exploded in the grounds unless the jury returned a guilty verdict.

Extra police were brought to the court and the double steel gates were locked for more than 30 minutes while security men and police checked the buildings. The jury was left inside during the search. Nothing was found and people were allowed to return to the court after everyone was searched by a metal detector at the gate and then again before entering the courtroom.

Police were pacing up and down as the jury considered their verdict. The Lynchs had gone home. Members of the public waited around the front fence. A few motorists blew their horns as they drove past. At 8.45pm, after nearly nine hours of deliberations, the court was recalled to inform everyone the jury had not reached a unanimous decision. They would have to stay out overnight and resume again in the morning. Justice Maxwell ordered total isolation of the jurors. No televisions, radios or newspapers and no contact with family unless through the assigned court officials. Six security staff were sworn in as "minders" for the group. Justice Maxwell apologised for the strict supervision and said he regretted the enforced isolation. The seven men and four women were driven to a city motel in a mini bus.

Next morning, Wednesday, June 10, 1987, the courtroom was packed. There wasn't an empty seat in the upstairs and ground floor public galleries. It was the first time the upstairs section had been open during this trial. Most police involved in the case attended, firstly out of duty — they wanted the result they believed in — secondly, out of respect for the Lynch family.

At 10.20am the jury informed Justice Maxwell they had reached a verdict. The atmosphere was electric. At 10.40pm the court was convened.

Journalists crammed along the benches especially set aside for them to the right of the prisoners, some kneeling in front of their colleagues because there was so little room. Burly police were squashed together in their area opposite, to the left of the dock. Garry and Grace Lynch sat quietly next to Anne Farmer. The enormous strain showed on their faces.

The jury filed into the crowded courtroom. Two jurors looked around. The others kept their heads down. Les Murphy's hands shook as he fiddled with a button on his shirt. His brother Gary smiled.

The grey-haired jury foreman in steel-framed glasses passed up a note to the Judge, informing him of the jury's decision on all 20 charges, five for each accused man. There was silence.

Then after each charge was read out against each of the four men the Judge asked, "Michael James Murdoch?"

"Guilty," said the foreman.

"Leslie Joseph Murphy?"

"Guilty."

"Michael Patrick Murphy?"

"Guilty."

"Gary Stephen Murphy?"

"Guilty."

Gary Murphy clenched his hands and looked down at the bench in front of him. Les Murphy stared blankly and gripped a plastic drinking cup. Michael Murphy looked at the floor then mouthed the words, "No, no." Murdoch almost disappeared from sight as he bowed his head.

There was a rush for the door as journalists on deadlines raced to be the first to report the news.

Guilty, Guilty, Guilty, Guilty. Two women jurors wiped tears from their eyes. Garry and Grace held hands, he nodding his head in appreciation. At the back of the court Gaynor Cobby wept. Rose Murdoch looked stunned and dabbed at her eyes. The police grinned. Even hardened journalists shed a tear or two for justice.

Bill Hosking called for a brief adjournment so he could receive some intructions from his client Michael Murphy. When the court resumed shortly after, the men's antecedents were read to the court. The job was Speed Kennedy's. Under oath he told the court the men had all been in custody for 15 months and had previously been associated with "a criminal element". As Kennedy's voice rang out, many jurors looked at each other. Les Murphy glared at them now. Gary Murphy continued conversation with his solicitor Leigh Johnson and Murdoch kept his head bowed. Michael Murphy gazed around the room.

Justice Maxwell refused a request by Marcus Bleasel for an adjournment to allow Murdoch to obtain a pre-sentence report. This report is often given in defence of a convicted person to outline reasons why he or she should have special circumstances taken into consideration. These range from why the prisoner should be placed in protective custody, receive a light sentence, have counselling, or how events in the past have contributed to the current crime. Alan

Saunders said any report would be "futile" in view of Murdoch's prior convictions. Sandy Wetmore said, "Gary Stephen Murphy maintains his innocence, he has nothing to say and he has no evidence to call." Mulligan said his client Les Murphy had instructed him to repeat his not guilty plea and said the conviction was disputed. Hosking added that Michael Murphy "likewise" maintains his innocence of the charges.

Justice Maxwell reassured the jury that their verdicts, in his view, were "proper" and he exempted them from jury service for 15 years. One of the women jurors sighed deeply.

The convicted men left the dock. Gary Murphy grinned as he headed down the wooden flight of stairs to the cells underneath. Murdoch turned and looked at his mother Rose, shrugging his shoulders before disappearing.

Les Murphy's girlfriend Nikki burst into tears as she ran down the court's driveway with a friend beside her. She was stopped by journalists at the big iron gates. "The system is wrong," she cried. "They are not guilty, they are not murderers!"

Chapter 35

Outside the court the Lynchs were beseiged by the media. Channel 7's Norm Lipson reached them first. He shepherded the couple down the driveway to a spot on the footpath next to his large outside broadcast van. He knew he would be first to get them to air in a live interview on the *Eleven AM* program, hosted by Don Willesee.

By now, nearly 50 TV, press and radio reporters had formed a ring around the couple. Shoppers, businessmen and people spilling out from the court stopped to watch the spectacle. Cars tooted their horns as they drove along Oxford St. Then Lipson's scheme came unstuck. There was a hitch at the studio, the link that would transmit the story had dropped out. This is every television producer's nightmare. Lipson tried to explain the problem quietly to the Lynchs. They all waited patiently.

Grace Lynch looked terrified as she stood next to her husband, surrounded by people wielding cameras, microphones, tape recorders and notebooks. Through the crowd she spotted a woman newspaper journalist who had become friendly with them, and looked across helplessly. This journalist worked her way closer and grabbed Grace's hand. She clutched it tightly while they waited patiently, surrounded by the crowd. Behind Grace Lynch was her friend, Anne Farmer. She had noticed the look on Grace's face too and now grabbed hold of her waist. The reporters were inching closer and the atmosphere was stifling. After four minutes, patience ran out. Angry journalists accused Lipson of hijacking the family. Just at that moment the go-ahead was given. The Lynchs finally spoke.

Garry Lynch explained that the family's decision to attend the trial was an important part of the grieving process for them. "We felt we just had to see those five," he said. "And we believed that once we had lived through the court case only then could we begin to put it all behind us and get on with our lives."

Grace Lynch continued: "We know some people must wonder how we could listen to the unspeakable things done to our daughter. But, you see, this case involved her too, and there was nobody in court to represent her. We're the only ones. So we went to court because we wanted to know things were being done properly. But if we hadn't gone we would have heard all those awful things second-hand at some stage. It would have hurt more and we didn't want that." She admitted there were times when it was difficult to listen to the recounting of the atrocities committed on Anita. "It's hard to realise there are such inhumane creatures in the world. They can't hurt our daughter anymore and they can't hurt us anymore. I just hope they realise the enormity of what they did to our family, to take a life . . . We can't ever forgive these five for what they did but we must stop hating them or that hatred will destroy us and the new hope we have found. It's up to God to punish them. Anita would not want us to look for vengeance."

Garry Lynch said he had hoped he would see the men show remorse for killing his daughter. "I have studied the five throughout the days in court and I have been looking hard for just a tiny thread of remorse from someone. Just something to show they were sorry for what they did. But I have seen nothing from any of them. Instead there has even been some sniggering. How do you rehabilitate people like this? I hope that when they are released they are old men. Then they won't be able to do these things to anybody."

Television reporters tried to question Les Murphy's girlfriend Nikki and her friend as they ran past Sgt Kennedy, who was speaking live to air to radio talk-back host John Laws. A tearful Nikki said, "It's completely unfair, no-one knows anything . . . the decision was wrong, completely wrong." Her friend, more composed, said, "I just think he's (Les) not guilty. They're human beings, everyone makes a mistake. They have just made a mistake that's bigger than other people's. You know, they've had a hard life."

Speed Kennedy told Channel 7 news reporter Felicity Moffatt that the difficulties of the case had set it aside from others he had worked on. At times, he said, many of the investigators found it difficult to control their feelings, particularly over allegations the killers were bashed by police. "There were times when one's anger might have come to the surface, compassion certainly for the family of the victim and anger, of course, when all the allegations were raised against us," Kennedy said. "But now that it's over we feel very justified that all the hard work and the criticisms levelled at us have been fought off and the right verdict has come through." With that, Kennedy called a halt to the media interviews. He had done about a dozen, one after the other. He was going for a beer with the boys.

A block away at the Gaslight Inn in Crown Street, Kennedy joined the rest of the investigators. "Mr Crown", prosecutor Alan Saunders, was there and he brought his hardworking solicitor Jenny Betts with him. Some court officials and Corrective Services officers even made it down. Some of the journalists were also there.

Later in the afternoon the drinkers shifted to the Macquarie Hotel in Wentworth Ave, a favourite watering hole of the police, because of its proximity to Police Headquarters a block away. They drank well into the afternoon. It was here that some of the difficulties of dealing with a high profile murder investigation emerged. Blacktown detective Paul Rynne began talking about how he had been unable to cope after seeing Anita Cobby lying in the Boiler Paddock in Reen Rd. The sight of her wounds had haunted him for months. Tears sprang to his eyes as he told of the post-mortem, where he saw the desecrated body of a beautiful young woman. The waste of life and how savagely it had been snatched was overwhelming, he said. The trauma had nearly cost him his marriage. He pulled out his wallet, displaying colour photos of his wife and smiling children. The tears welled again in his big eyes when he admitted he had been unable to make love to his wife for almost three months after the post-mortem. "Every time I even thought about it I could see Mrs Cobby and all her injuries," Rynne said. "(During the investigation) I used to get out of bed at night and just sit on the back porch looking at the stars thinking, 'Anita, you're up there and you know who did this to you. There must be some way you can let us know. Give us some sort of a clue.'" He needed the comfort of his family but instead had to spend long hours working on the case. When he was at home, "all I could think about was Anita and what they had done to her."

Several months after the trial Const Rynne was put on indefinite sick leave — stress related — due mainly to the Anita Cobby investigation, doctors ruled. In 1989, Paul Rynne was pensioned out of the police force because of stress. He hadn't returned to full-time duties since the end of the Anita Cobby trial.

After the guilty verdict the four men returned to the 5-cell protection block in Five-Wing at Parklea Prison which they shared with John Travers. Shortly after their return, a scuffle broke out between the five and three police officers had to step in and break it up.

The protection wing at the prison allowed inmates to share a private exercise yard and use a communal room which had a set of weights in it. It was specifically designed to separate the mainstream of around 200 prisoners from the handful whose lives had been threatened. Also in the same wing at this time were international drug smugglers Barry Ball and Bruce "Snapper" Cornwell.

Chapter 36

The day after the conviction of the Cobby killers, stories surfaced about contracts being taken out on their lives. Keeping the killers safe in prison was always going to be difficult. Reports of attacks against them had circulated from the time they were charged. Some were substantiated, others couldn't be confirmed. It was said the men had had their food urinated on, their drinks spat in, their court clothes changed around or taken and their cells turned upside down. Prison officers said on one occasion water was thrown over two of the men as they walked past the cells on their way to the trial.

One morning Les Murphy turned up at court several hours late after supposedly being hit by a steel door on his way out of the prison van. Prison officers said the real story was Murphy had been knocked unconscious by another prisoner. In any case he was pale when he arrived at court and his solicitor asked for a doctor to be called because he was suffering from headaches and dizziness.

Another incident, mentioned in court, was when Gary Murphy suffered what was said to be an epileptic fit. His face, body and legs were bruised and his chest and back had cuts across them as if slashed with a razor blade. He said he remembered nothing about it.

Then, Michael Murphy arrived hours late to be sentenced for escaping from Silverwater Gaol. His solicitor asked that he be allowed to sit for the whole proceedings because of a "painful lower back problem". Murphy looked pale and sick. Privately, it was said he had been attacked by another prisoner, who had forced a piece of plastic piping into his anus. Inside the tubing had been a section of barbed wire, which was left exposed when the tubing was pulled away.

John Travers has been the target of several attacks, the worst in January, 1990, when he needed hospital treatment after being knocked to the ground in a fight he provoked with another inmate. Sharon Travers once told a television host she expected her son to die in gaol. "I wait for the time when I wake up and turn on the telly to find out that someone's got to him," she said. "When I visit him prisoners yell things at you when they know who you are visiting. They have said, 'You won't have to visit him much longer.'"

The five have not been model inmates. Two of the Murphys tested positive to marijuana during a drug test at Long Bay Gaol in 1988. Michael Murdoch was questioned with three others about the sexual assault of a 19-year-old mentally handicapped prisoner in Long Bay and Gary Murphy has been involved in several brawls, one defending a prison nurse who had been sworn at by another inmate. The prisoner suffered a broken jaw after Murphy hit him about 15 times during the attack on January 11, 1990. That added another conviction and a two-year sentence to Murphy's file.

The men today are not friends. Michael Murphy won't communicate with Les Murphy or Murdoch, while Travers keeps to himself. Les Murphy said in 1990 that he wanted nothing more to do with Murdoch because he believed he'd helped police by turning informant. "When I was being taken on the run-around I looked over to the right of me and saw Murdoch through a window smiling with one of the coppers. He didn't see me," Murphy said in Long Bay prison.

The Corrective Services Department has tried to minimise the attention paid to the notorious five men. Scores of journalists have requested interviews with them but all have been turned down. One Corrective Services official explained the policy was to keep the killers as far from the public eye as possible. "We want them to just settle down and serve their time. They are not stars. They will never be allowed to conduct interviews with the media under any circumstances while the Liberal Government rules NSW. It's purely for the reason that Anita Cobby's family has suffered enough. These men don't deserve the attention. They are killers."

After the trial, though, the threats against the lives of Travers, Murdoch and the three Murphys became more intense. Prison officials acknowledged security for the men would be a problem, because of the unprecedented publicity surrounding the case. Already they were being held in segregated protective custody sections in

Long Bay and Parklea prisons. The day after their convictions for murder, Federal President of the Prison Officers Association Pat Armstrong confirmed the five wouldn't be put in the prison mainstream for at least five years. "It's the hope that after five years or more other prisoners might have forgotten what they did and the grudges held against them," Armstrong said. "After that the prison authorities will probably try to slot them back in the prison system." But the controversy continued when it was disclosed the cost of keeping a prisoner in protective custody each year was around $40,000.

The TV, radio and press wrap-up stories at the end of the trial were dramatic. Radio stations ran interviews with anyone remotely connected with the case. One station broadcast a half-hour special. The media hunt for the families of the men was on. Sharon Travers hadn't been seen in public. In fact she had only attended court on two occasions after the men were first charged and then the media didn't know who she was. Channel 7 secured her for an interview. News reporter Kaye Brown won her over. At their first meeting Sharon Travers was shaking. Her hair was oily and messy and her eyes were red. Tears often rolled down her cheeks while she talked, no matter how hard she tried to control them. She dabbed her eyes and blew her nose with a yellow tissue. She agreed to appear on the *Terry Willesee Tonight* program and despite the desperate pleas from her son not to, the interview went ahead. Again she tried to contain her emotions as she talked about her son and the murder of Anita Cobby.

Les and Dulcie Murphy were not sighted during the entire 16 months and Danny Murphy was the only family representative to attend the committal proceedings. At various times, friends and girlfriends of the accused were there, but not regularly, and the media was never sure who they were. Only Rose Murdoch attended every day of court, mostly with her daughters and sometimes with a female companion.

Again, Norm Lipson outdid his rivals with a recorded interview with Garry and Grace Lynch and their daughter Kathryn. In it Lipson used a home video of Anita as a toddler, playing at the water's edge on a beach, running around a Hill's Hoist, smiling on a rocking horse and sitting on her grandfather's knee. She had a mop of blonde curls and a face glowing with the innocence of childhood. In the background played the song the Lynchs had heard on *The Midday Show* on the day Anita's body was found, *If You Go Away*. It was moving stuff and even the TV tape editor who put the story together became emotional when working on it. News producers cried at the station the night it went to air.

The newspaper coverage was intense. The Anita Cobby story dominated the papers for days and the public consumed every word. Every time an article on Anita Cobby was printed, newspaper circulation increased. Even a story about Anita's dog, Lucy, that so fretted for its mistress that it had to be put down, made the front page of the paper. That was indicative of the wide interest this woman's life and death commanded.

Chapter 37

The following week, on Tuesday, June 16, 1987, the five men were sentenced. Sydney bus driver Jackson Mashinini, who had taken up his position in the court's public gallery that day, was a modern-day town crier, the first with the news. With the details of the sentencing fresh in his mind and a wide grin on his face, Mashinini bounded out of the courtroom and down the driveway, stopping briefly as he reached the footpath to announce to the world, "Never to be released!" In his blue uniform and cap he was off again, running back to his Urban Transit Authority bus he'd parked in Oxford St outside the court on his way to work. He didn't have time to hang around.

As he left, the crowd of 30 or so gathered outside the court gates repeated his words, "Never to be released", patting each other on the back and shaking hands. It was as if each had won his or her own personal victory.

At 8.30 that morning people had begun standing outside the court waiting for the gates to open half an hour later. When they did, some sprinted to the front of the huge metal doors of courtroom No.5 and formed a queue. By 9.45am when the courtroom doors opened, 150 were waiting in the light rain to go inside to claim their seats. Rose Murdoch kept her usual spot in the middle row of the gallery, almost directly behind her son. Garry and Grace Lynch were absent that day but were represented by Anne Farmer and her son. The Lynchs had left the previous day for a break and were in Albury that morning.

After seven minutes the courtroom was filled. Officials opened up the very rarely used top gallery to ease the congestion. No-one knew where all the people had come from. Most hadn't known Anita Cobby, but they all wanted to see these men punished.

One middle-aged man walked up and down the courthouse

driveway with a yellow cardboard sign. It read, "I refuse to pay taxes to keep these mongrels in gaol. Hang them, but flog them first."

At 10.17, the Judge began his summation of the trial evidence. Reading the charges and the maximum penalties carried by each, Justice Maxwell said, ". . . the charges to which (the prisoner Travers) pleaded guilty to are as follows that: "Under section 19 of the Crimes Act, on the second day of February, 1986 at Prospect in NSW he did murder Anita Lorraine Cobby. Penalty, penal servitude for life.

"Under section 90a of the Crimes Act on the second day in February, 1986, at Blacktown in NSW, he did take away Anita Lorraine Cobby with intent to hold Anita Lorraine Cobby for advantage. The maximum penalty, penal servitude for 20 years.

"Under section 96 of the Crimes Act, on the second day of February, 1986. at Blacktown in NSW, he did assault Anita Lorraine Cobby and rob her of certain property, to wit, one bag, one purse and a quantity of clothing, and immediately after robbing the said Anita Lorraine Cobby, did use other corporal violence to the said Anita Lorraine Cobby, thereby wounding the said, Anita Lorraine Cobby. The maximum penalty, penal servitude for life.

"Under section 61c of the Crimes Act, on the second day of February, 1986, at Prospect in NSW he maliciously did inflict actual bodily harm upon Anita Lorraine Cobby with intent to have sexual intercourse with the said Anita Lorraine Cobby. Maximum penalty, penal servitude for 12 years.

"Under section 117 of the Crimes Act, on or about the 28th day of January, 1986, at Seven Hills in NSW, he did steal a Holden sedan, the property of Bruce Anthony Commins. The maximum penalty, penal servitude for five years."

Justice Maxwell explained that each of the four men whose cases went to trial before a jury faced the same charges as Travers with the exception of Leslie Murphy who was charged separately with stealing the same car under sub-section 117/154a of the Crimes Act.

"The Crown case was that the prisoners, including the prisoner Travers, were at the relevant time combining together in order to effect a common criminal purpose," Justice Maxwell said. "So far as the first charge of murder is concerned, although it is common ground that the prisoner Travers killed the deceased, the Crown deemed it proper to charge the other four with having committed the same murder . . . firstly the Crown alleged that after having assaulted and robbed the deceased and sexually assaulting her by having intercourse anally, orally and vaginally against her will, they were conscious of the fact she could recognise them and they therefore agreed she should be killed."

The second of the Crown's points, he said, was "each of the accused was aware that the prisoner Travers was armed with a knife so each of them contemplated that it might be used by Travers with the intention of killing or causing grievous bodily harm to the deceased . . . it suffices to say that the jury accepted one or both the points upon which the Crown presented its first charge against the prisoners."

Justice Maxwell then presented a summary of the facts relating to Anita Cobby's last known movements and the events of her abduction, assault, murder and her injuries. ". . . what the doctor (Malouf) saw on her body by way of contusions and bruises was consistent with a systematic beating. There was also evidence there had been anal intercourse. One cannot establish precisely the length of time that she was subjected to the attacks giving rise to the wounds . . . but it is open on the evidence to conclude that it was upwards of at least an hour and a half." He then outlined how the men left their victim to die, returning to Travers' home where Anita's clothes were burnt and the ashes disposed of.

"There is no doubt that apart from the humiliation, degradation and terror inflicted upon this poor young woman, she was the victim of a prolonged and sadistic physical and sexual assault, including repeated assaults, orally, anally and vaginally. Wild animals are given to pack assaults and killings. However, they do so for the purpose of survival and not as a result of a degrading animal's passion. Not so these prisoners. They assaulted in a pack for the purpose of satisfying their lust and killed for the purpose of identification." Justice Maxwell appeared to have tears in his eyes. He was offered a glass of water and sipped from it before continuing.

"This is one of the most horrifying physical and sexual assaults I have encountered in my 40-odd years associated with the law. The crime is exacerbated by the fact that the victim almost certainly was made aware, in the end, of her pending death.

"Throughout the long trial the prisoners, albeit to a lesser degree in the case of Murdoch, showed no signs of remorse or contrition. Indeed they were observed to be laughing with one another and frequently were seen to be sniggering behind their hands."

At 10.41am he ordered the prisoners to stand while the brief details about each of their backgrounds and criminal records were read out. Everyone remained silent and still. Then, "Having regard to the circumstances of these crimes and of the prisoners, I find it difficult to differentiate between them in fact and in law. I also take into account the fact that the first four crimes were committed as part and parcel of one, albeit horrifying, episode . . . against Anita Cobby." He said that no submissions had been made on their behalf and no evidence was before him to suggest any mitigating circumstances, significantly reducing the culpability of the men's involvement in the crimes. But there had been such a submission for John Travers, based upon two pyschiatric reports by Dr Hugh Jolly and another by a consulting psychologist, Dr Geoffrey Fox.

In his reports, which were accepted into evidence, Dr Jolly said, "In the period leading up to the killing, Travers lived a half-crazed, reckless sort of life, intoxicated with this and that, aggressive, paranoid and very unstable." In assessing Travers he found "under certain circumstances, he can be paranoid and 'real violent'. He will hit people when he 'don't give a fuck about nothing' but I would not say he was suffering a major psychiatric illness, meaning that he is not grossly psychotic."

Dr Jolly said he could find no history of a severe head injury to Travers (that could be given as an excuse for his behaviour) but Travers had told him "he had been knocked unconscious once when he caught his jeans on a fence (obviously when he was breaking in somewhere) and he landed on his head on the concrete. In similar circumstances he cut his throat at the age of 15 or so, trying to get in somewhere, but there is no evidence of any gross brain damage. He says he has had no serious illness as a child — after his tonsils were taken out, he then 'never seen a doctor for years'. He even fractured a collarbone but didn't go to the doctor because he didn't like the treatment he'd had earlier.

"In his short life, Mr Travers has ingested most of the drugs which would have been socially available, either legally or illegally." Travers told Dr Jolly that on the morning of the murder he had been drinking at home and later went to the Plumpton Hotel and later continued drinking at home with a case of beer. "It sounded to me as if Mr Travers drank heavily and smoked a lot of marijuana that day although he cannot give me exact quantities. He talked about 'half an ounce' . . . he only has islands of memory after that . . . he says he 'spun out' and heard the instructions 'Trawney, do your stuff'. He is adamant he heard these words — 'something that stuck in my head.' He understands it was wrong to have killed her and he said 'I just know that I done it . . . I get most of it back from dreams...you gotta block things out . . . you got to . . . If you can't do it you won't survive . . .' I believe the memory of having done this deed greatly bothers Mr Travers."

Dr Jolly said, "Travers acknowledges that he becomes very aggressive when drunk. He 'don't care about myself, don't care about anything . . . every day you'd find enough money to get a couple of goons . . . that went on for donkeys' . . . there were 'heaps of parties that have lasted a week'."

Travers' closeness to his maternal grandmother who "was me mother to me" was evident, Dr Jolly said and after she died three years before the killing from terminal cancer Travers found it difficult to come to terms with . . . it seems to me that her loss was the trigger to the acting of all sorts of destructive feelings . . . I think he hurt someone quiet badly after her death, hitting someone with a piece of plastic covered pipe because he said he 'had to let it out'. From shortly after his grandmother's death it is my assessment that Mr Travers became markedly paranoid."

Although Dr Jolly made it clear he didn't espouse the "unhappy childhood" situation in absolving individuals from responsibility for their actions as adults, he said ". . . the harm done to Mr Travers when he was a child almost certainly, bit by bit, led to the present situation . . . it does seem to me that Mr Travers was beaten into a situation where insecure aggression was his only coping mechanism against a (perceived) hostile world.

". . . In clear consciousness, detoxified, Mr Travers is really quite a pleasant man. It may be difficult for some people to accept that. As he said to me 'I want to lead a simple life...fish, hunt, travel, make friends . . . I don't make friends very easily.' He is not of the psychotic disposition which is immune to the harm it does to other people. He does not take pleasure in hurting other living creatures. There is no doubt in my mind he feels considerable regret and remorse . . . In my view he is not a lost cause . . ."

Justice Maxwell referred to two extracts from Dr Jolly's second report on Travers in which he says, "I suppose a decision as to whether there are exculpating factors depends on whether or not it is believed Mrs Cobby was killed in cold blood, as it were, in order that she might not later identify her attackers." And the second ". . . I do not believe he acted cold-bloodedly, or reasoning in clear consciousness towards his self preservation."

Justice Maxwell then told the court,"My perusal of all the relevant evidence does not dissuade me to this finding. Indeed I find to the contrary. This was a calculated killing — done in cold blood . . . therefore, I impose the following sentences."

Everyone was silent. You could hear people breathing. Justice Maxwell said, "John Raymond Travers, Michael James Murdoch, Leslie Joseph Murphy, Gary Steven Murphy and Michael Patrick Murphy, on the second count of abduction, I sentence you each to penal servitude for 16 years." The men remained still in the dock and the gallery was equally still. "On the third count of assault and rob with wounding, I sentence you each to penal servitude for 17 years. On the fourth count of maliciously inflicting actual bodily harm with intent to have sexual intercourse, I sentence you each to penal servitude for 12 years. On the fifth count of larceny of a motor vehicle, John Raymond Travers, Michael James Murdoch, Michael Patrick Murphy and Gary Steven Murphy, I sentence you each to penal servitude for five years. Leslie Joseph Murphy, I sentence you to penal servitude of three years."

His Honour then told the court the sentences were to be served from the time the men were taken into custody. For Travers that was February 21, 1986, Murdoch, Gary and Leslie Murphy were to commence theirs from February 24, 1986, and Michael Murphy's new sentences were to begin at the expiration of the ones he was serving, when he escaped from Silverwater prison.

Justice Maxwell had kept the charge of murder until last. The five prisoners remained silently in the dock. His Honour continued. "John Raymond Travers, Michael James Murdoch, Leslie Joseph Murphy, Michael Patrick Murphy and Gary Steven Murphy, on the first count of murder I sentence you each to penal servitude for life." It had been expected. There was a buzz of soft chatter and movement around the courtroom. The five men all stared ahead, betraying no emotion.

Justice Maxwell proceeded, "The circumstances of these prisoners and the circumstances of the murder of Anita Lorraine Cobby prompt me to recommend that the official files of each prisoner should be clearly marked, 'Never to be released'." This was unexpected. And so was the response. With those words, "Never to be released", the room erupted into spontaneous applause. The atmosphere was euphoric as people clapped, cheered and even whistled. Not one of the prisoners looked around but John Travers rolled his eyes towards the ceiling. At that point, one of the Murphys later said he thought people would jump the dock and head for them.

The pandemonium could be heard in other courtrooms, outside, across the street, even above the busy morning traffic. It startled the police working in the main office in the adjoining building. "I've never heard such a thing happening in a court before and I've been here a long time," said one middle-aged court official. Court officers moved quickly around the court, demanding order. It came about a minute later.

Justice Maxwell took a deep breath, a sip of water from his glass, and swallowed hard. He was unimpressed by the reaction in his courtroom. "If there is any more of that I will clear the court," he said, and continued, "If the Executive deems it proper in the future to consider their file, then I would echo the advice proferred, in a case in which the facts were not entirely dissimilar, by a former and distinguished Chief Judge at Common Law, namely, that the Executive should grant to the prisoners the same degree of mercy that they bestowed upon Anita Lorraine Cobby in the Boiler Paddock, Prospect, on the night of February 2, 1986. I do not think the public would expect otherwise."

Outside, Anne Farmer said she believed the Lynchs would be elated when news of the sentencing reached them. "You can't have these sort of people out on the streets. They will also be happy to know how emotional the people in the public gallery were." Her son, Anita's old boyfriend, was visibly moved. In front of the court, standing in the light rain, he found every one of the investigators. With tears in his eyes, his voice sometimes breaking, he said, "Thanks mate" as he shook their hands. "Well done."

Les Murphy's girlfriend Nikki walked from the courtroom in tears. She told waiting newsmen, "I think the sentence sucks, it really sucks. I only hope they go better in their appeal." Almost as an afterthought, she said that Anita Cobby shouldn't have been walking home that night. "Everyone knows how bad Blacktown is. I wouldn't even walk around at night where I live and that is an upper-class suburb." Another female friend of Les Murphy was still defending him. "They were all drunk, they were all stoned. I have sympathy for the family but that doesn't mean I have to run around like everyone else and say, 'hang the bastards'."

Detective Kennedy said it was "a fair indication of the pressure everyone has been under during this trial, when the Judge got upset reading a section of his judgement. I'm really glad it is all over." Graham Rosetta was brief in his comments. "Justice has been done." Kevin Raue said the result was justified "after a combined effort by police, the media and the community".

Rose Murdoch wept outside the court. She told journalists she was "heartbroken" with the decision. She said she still believed Michael was innocent. "I feel I've lost a son. I'm angry that it ever happened. He's been a special boy to me and still is. There's no way he had anything to do with Anita's murder." She said she didn't believe in capital punishment. "The public want them to swing, to castrate them. They think they should hang. I don't believe in it and it's not right in this case. There's been so much bad publicity. There's got to be something good come out of this, there has to."

At Parliament House, NSW Premier Barrie Unsworth said, "These men will never be on the streets again as far as I'm concerned."

For Justice Maxwell, this day signalled the end of months of enormous pressure. Very few people were aware of the anguish he experienced during this trial. His emotions had surfaced only briefly during the sentencing. Television reporter Felicity Moffatt filmed the

Judge that afternoon in his city office overlooking Hyde Park and St Mary's Cathederal. Trying to make conversation with His Honour, she asked if he was glad the trial was over. "Yes, very" was his reply. Again, she reminded him of how he seemed to choke with emotion during the delivery of the sentence and he shrugged it off, saying, "Oh, I just had a hiccup, that's all."

As the killers were escorted back to Parklea Gaol, a group of 10 demonstrators vented their feelings by bashing on the prison van as it pulled out from the back of the court complex. "You bastards, you'll die before your time!" yelled one man, while a woman screamed, "I hope you rot in there."

When the men were safely back in the segregated protection unit of the prison, they stood around in the small exercise yard. One prison officer remembered how Travers was in shock at the sentence he received. "He was stunned and staring, as if he couldn't blink," the officer said. "His mind was a million miles away. One of the others called out to him and he glared back, said a few sharp words and walked away."

Chapter 38

The next day, Wednesday, June 17, 1987, Raymond John Paterson stood trial before Justice Maxwell in the same court where the five men had been sentenced to life for killing Anita Cobby. Paterson pleaded not guilty to two charges of being an accessory after the fact of Anita Cobby's murder by receiving, harbouring and assisting Michael and Gary Murphy knowing they were involved in the murder. He had been on bail for the 16 months since he was charged.

In the first record of interview, Det Phil Gaspert said Paterson was shaking and sweating while he typed up the questions and answers. Paterson admitted to police on February 21, 1986, that he knew that a car which Gary Murphy had left at his place had had its number plates changed and had been resprayed. But he denied knowledge that it had been used in the Anita Cobby murder.

However, a few days later, when police returned to question him again, Paterson admitted to Kennedy he had lent his car to Gary Murphy after he had dumped the stolen car and burnt it. He said the stolen car had been repainted undercoat grey at the home of a man named Phillip. "I think it was a bluey-grey colour, with blue interior and no bumper bar," Paterson said. He still denied knowing the car had been used to abduct Anita Cobby or that the men had killed her. This admission by Paterson was considered a breakthrough for police. Knowing Gary Murphy had burnt the car was extremely significant. Paterson had agreed to show police where he thought the car had been dumped. The car wasn't found. He said he knew Travers through Les and Gary Murphy and only knew Murdoch as someone who frequently smoked marijuana and drank.

After Murdoch, Travers and Les Murphy had been brought in for questioning for car stealing, Paterson was re-interviewed by Chris O'Toole and Hugh Dundas, who took a second record of interview on February 24. He was then charged with being an accessory after the murder. This time Paterson admitted he had lied about his knowledge of the car after being threatened by the men. He said Gary Murphy was not a violent person but that Travers and Murdoch might have been because Murphy had told him they were both mad.

Now, he said that on the night the car was burnt, the night after the murder, Gary Murphy told him the front brakes on the stolen car were "buggered" and rather than fix them he would burn the car to get rid of the fingerprints. When the men came back Gary Murphy had told him the car "went up real good and I heard the fire brigade". Paterson said, "It was roughly around midnight when they got back." It was this night, Paterson said, when the men had told him they had "killed a woman, mutilated her". He said they didn't tell him where the woman had been killed, "but I knew it a couple of days later when I heard it on the radio. I was real scared. I didn't know what to do so I didn't do anything." That night Mick and Gary Murphy had stayed in Paterson's loungeroom.

Ray Paterson was convicted on two charges of being an accessory after the fact of murder and for harbouring, assisting and maintaining Gary and Michael Murphy.

In a pre-sentence report, Justice Maxwell heard Paterson had criminal tendencies but was not addicted to alcohol or drugs. He had only minor convictions — for speeding and driving while unlicensed and uninsured in 1972, stealing and larceny of two motor vehicles in 1982 and stealing in a retail store in 1984. Police said at his trial Paterson had also given information that helped in a "breakthrough" in the murder investigation. The Judge heard that Paterson was semi-illiterate after leaving school at 14 and of a probation report that said, "All reports indicate that when in the wrong company the offender is easily led astray. Family members expressed the belief that Mr Paterson's friends regularly 'take advantage' of his helpful nature."

Justice Maxwell told the court, "I must steel myself against being influenced by the knowledge of the treatment and the manner of death of Anita Lorraine Cobby." He sentenced Paterson to eight years gaol with a three year non-parole period.

Mavis Leanne Saunders and Debra Jane McAskill were

charged with being accessories after the fact of murder. They admitted to police they knew Michael and Gary Murphy were being sought for the murder of Anita Cobby yet failed to notify police. The women pleaded not guilty and were acquitted. Saunders was convicted on a charge of harbouring and given a good behaviour bond.

When Ray Paterson was released from prison on March 22, 1989, after serving only 21 months of his eight-year sentence, there was a public outcry. He was released from Cooma gaol, a medium security prison, following a decision by the NSW Parole Board. The State Corrective Services Minister, Michael Yabsley, slammed the decision to allow Paterson to be released before the recommended three-year non-parole period was up. " I am appalled," Yabsley said and then described the administration of sentencing in NSW as "a nonsense of the worst kind." He said the Government had no say at all in what the Parole Board did.

At the time of Paterson's release the NSW Government had a proposal about to go before the Cabinet requiring prisoners to serve at least 75 per cent of their total sentences. "In Paterson's case, under this scheme, he would have to serve six years of the eight year sentence," Yabsley said. That legislation has since been introduced.

Paterson has made just one public appearance to speak about his involvement in the Anita Cobby murder. Several months after his release, Paterson was interviewed for Channel Nine's *A Current Affair* program and said, "I wish I'd never met 'em (Travers, Murdoch and the three Murphys)." His conviction, he said, had broken up his marriage and he'd lost his three children.

Paterson said he often thought of the torment and trauma Anita Cobby must have gone through at the hands of the men and the anguish of her family. "I am deeply sorry for what happened to their daughter. I want them to know that I am sorry and that I had nothing to do with it."

Chapter 39

The week after the men began their life sentences, Miss X spoke publicly for the first time about her role in catching the killers. Again, it was a coup for *The Sun*, the Sydney afternoon tabloid. Police roundsman Simon Bouda was the only one who managed to penetrate the tight net of security for an interview. Bouda remembered the extraordinary lengths he went to to get the interview. "The paper had to hire a motel room and have it checked out by SWOS for security reasons," Bouda said. "My credentials had to be examined through my contacts with Homicide police and strict instructions were laid down about the taping of the interview. They were so concerned for her safety. Her minder was with her all the time. We couldn't take photographs of her face and I couldn't describe her features. We had to photograph her from behind and silhouette her profile. I remember I shook her hand and there was a slight tremor down her arm that passed into mine. It was sheer terror. She was shaking and smoked constantly. She really didn't relax, fearing for her life.

"As we started talking she opened up. I believe she really cared for John Travers — a guardian-type relationship where she tried to have a good influence over his life. At times she was near tears, the emotion of going through it again."

Bouda asked her whether she thought the recommendation that the men never be released was a good idea. Miss X replied, "Maybe not so good for young Mick but then again I suppose the court knows best."

Bouda: "What about John?"

Miss X: "Definitely, there will be no recovery for him."

Bouda: "Were you surprised John pleaded guilty to the charges?"

Miss X: "I hoped he would, I really hoped he would. Well, we had him cold. There was no use saying anything else. I admire him for it. I really do."

She talked openly about the reintroduction of capital punishment in Australia, saying, "Nobody has the right to murder. Nobody has the right to take a life and I feel (if you do) you should pay with your own life. If you're prepared to take somebody else's life, be prepared to have yours taken. You can't have people like that in society. I don't believe that there is any rehabilitation for people like that. I feel John is capable of going (killing) again. Put him out of his misery."

Shortly after that interview, Miss X and her family packed up their belongings and said goodbye to Sydney. The Witness Protection Program deemed it impossible for her to stay in the city. They all had to be moved away. Now she says that is one of the things she regrets about the whole incident. "I loved Australia. I really wanted to stay there but that has all changed now. There are too many bad memories to go back. It really is the land of opportunity, there the world is at your feet and when I came, I had a better way of life and I knew the sky was the limit. That's why I feel cheated I can't live there anymore. I didn't do anything wrong but I still keep paying. My family still keeps paying. It's like a fairytale gone wrong."

It was the Cobby case that paved the way for the streamlining of the Witness Protection Program in NSW. In fact, caring for Miss X and her young family became a test case for the specialist unit. Never before had NSW police had a civilian case of this complexity. Usually police were either looking after politicians or visiting dignitaries or police informants with drug or underworld connections. This time their witness had to be protected 24 hours a day, she had to be relocated and, after appearing in court, be relocated yet again with her family. Each family member had to be given a new name and identity. So tight was the veil of secrecy around Miss X, that even members of the investigating team didn't know where she was. They couldn't even contact her without going through the Witness Protection Unit and, then, only a handful of people there knew where she was. After ironing out a few problems, members of the Unit believe the system is now foolproof.

Chapter 40

The three Murphys and Murdoch lodged appeals against their convictions. Travers appealed against the severity of his sentence, but later withdrew the appeal. The other appeals were dismissed except for Les Murphy's. Murphy claimed he was present when Anita Cobby was killed but did not participate. The High Court granted him a retrial on the grounds that a psychologist report that stated his mental capabilities were those of a 10-year-old wasn't allowed in evidence in the first trial by Justice Maxwell.

When the appeal was being heard in the High Court, Crown solicitor Jenny Betts had to be taken home, ill. Very few solicitors knew the trial evidence as well as she. In her absence the court was inadvertently led to believe the only evidence against Leslie Murphy was his disputed record of interview which was incorrect. On that erroneous belief the five judges voted 3-2 in favour of the previous conviction being quashed and that a new trial be granted to Murphy.

The retrial began in courtroom No.5 at Darlinghurst on July 8, 1990. This time Les Murphy looked better. Again he wore a cream V-neck woollen jumper and a brown bomber jacket, as he had in the first trial three years before. But this time he was suntanned, was a little heavier and he wore his hair parted down the middle in a slicked-back 1930s style. His shoulders and arms had built up, no doubt from his daily routine of running and gym work. He still moved his lips when reading. He craned his neck from side to side as if he had a problem with it.

The hype and publicity surrounding the first trial was absent this time. Very few of the media attended the hearing, partly due to the number of other important cases elsewhere around the city. Now, the faces of the reporters were young and unfamiliar.

The evidence of psychiatrist Ricky Sharpe that Murphy's comprehension wasn't of an adult standard was expected to work in his favour. His lawyer, Sandy Wetmore, claimed Murphy couldn't have understood all the questions put to him in the records of interview. In fact, Murphy claimed the answers weren't even his.

However the jury was shown sections of a previous record of interview with police in 1982, in which Murphy had used many of the words his counsel now claimed he would not have understood in 1986. The jurors were unaware of the context of the interview and they were told to disregard the fact he had even spoken to police. In that record of interview he had pleaded guilty, accepted the statement, and claimed he understood every word it contained, including some of the ones he was now disputing. What the jury wasn't told was that the passage was taken from a record of interview where Murphy admitted to the sexual assault of a 14-year-old girl in Hyde Park.

The jury deliberated for nine hours and, as in the first trial, asked for several sections of the evidence to be re-read. But, again, the jury found him guilty of the murder of Anita Cobby. Justice Badgery Parker sentenced him immediately to life imprisonment. However he declined to mark Murphy's papers "Never to be released", as Justice Maxwell had done in the previous trial. Under new sentencing laws passed in 1989 by the New South Wales Government, a convicted person must serve the full term of imprisonment. A life sentence is exactly that. This new law is known as "truth in sentencing". Murphy was sent back to Long Bay Gaol to serve his sentence.

Being called to Sydney for Murphy's retrial was a shock to Miss X. After adjusting to a new life, she had put the whole Cobby nightmare behind her. But after three years the emotion remained. In the witness box the memory of her role as a police informant came flooding back. She again shook while she gave evidence and she shed a tear when remembering the moment John Travers confessed to the killing.

Miss X believes that Travers probably has never come to terms with why he did the things he did. "I've had time to think about it and there was an underlying factor which I don't think even John realised was there," she said. "I shouldn't speak ill of the dead, but

John may have been getting back at women because of his mother. The way she had been in the home, the things he told me had happened to him as a child. He loved his mum but it was almost as if in defiance of her."

Her views on capital punishment remain unchanged and she is adamant it's the correct punishment for serious crimes. "This crime has been cruel to Anita Cobby's parents," Miss X said. "Our laws here must be changed. Anita Cobby went through hours of torture and if our public knew just what she suffered then they would insist that these sick animals be put down. They kill dogs when they bite . . . No-one has the right to do what they have done, to end a life . . . they have lost their right to life and have to die."

Miss X paused and there was a certain sadness in her voice. "I still haven't come to terms with it. I can't accept that John, someone I knew and loved, has done this terrible thing even though I know he did do it. What I can't handle is that the Lynchs seem to have no animosity, they are so prepared to forgive them. I can't and it wasn't even my child. I still care about John and I wish I could say something to him. I feel I owe him an explanation. But I don't really. I would say, 'I'm sorry, it just had to be.' I'm sorry for his life, that it couldn't have been better."

In the three years she has been away from Sydney, Miss X's family's lifestyle has changed dramatically. They have had time to start again. "We've totally relocated. We have no past. We're all very careful about what we say. We have two years of our lives that we just don't talk about. We have to keep it up, it's protecting ourselves. My husband works for cash, we have changed our names, it's like we've been born again and we've shut the doors on the old life to start a new and better one. If anything, this has taught my children to be sensitive and they are pacifists. I will not allow my kids to wear black T-shirts or sweat shirts. John always liked dark colours. My family wears happy warm colours and that's the sort of people we are. My kids went through so much. But I would do it all again."

Miss X was cautious when speaking of her share of the $100,000 reward posted by the NSW Government for the conviction of Anita Cobby's killers. One Government official told journalists, "It wasn't as much as you think she would have received. There were others who received a share." Those "others" were a group of four people who assisted police during the investigation. None of them were called to give evidence. Their identities have been kept secret to protect them. Maxine Greensmith was not among the rewardees. Miss X said her portion of the reward money had helped her buy a home. "Buying a house was the start of rebuilding our lives," she said. "But no amount is enough compensation for the hell we all went through. I don't regret doing what I did because I was right. I consider myself an upstanding citizen in the community."

Chapter 41

After the killers were sentenced, *The Daily Mirror* set to work on an exclusive interview with John Cobby, Anita's estranged husband. After painstakingly tracking him down through friends, relatives and associates, *Mirror* news editor John Choueifate contacted him. Cobby agreed to an interview, "a once-only story". It was a coup for the *Mirror*. Cobby had been silent. He had never once spoken to the media. He had disappeared after his wife was killed. Even many close friends didn't know what had happened to him. "He was very cautious about the media when I first got in touch with him," Choueifate said. "He had changed his name, the people where he worked didn't know his real identity and he was fiercely protective of his privacy only because he didn't think he'd be able to cope if people knew who he was." So secret was the series, that less than six people at the paper knew it was being done. The story was written on a special computer with a security code and was kept hidden until the last minute before going to press. The *Mirror* sent Cobby and his sister Gaynor into hiding on the Gold Coast with Choueifate as minder while the publicity machine was cranked up. After months of planning and weeks of working with John Cobby, the story, by Mark Morri, was published.

Devastated by his wife's death, Cobby had fled to America to stay with a friend. The murder changed his life. He drank more, he became aggressive, he couldn't sleep and he lost interest in his friends. He couldn't watch a TV, listen to a radio or read a newspaper because of his great fear of hearing about the case. Even his family was shocked at his haggard appearance. He couldn't cope, and despite sedation, he had nightmares every night. He would wake from his sleep in a cold sweat after dreaming he had killed the five men who raped, tortured and murdered his beloved Anita. "In this subconscious ritual he executes the men over and over again. He hangs, then shoots them and stabs them . . . then he wakes exhausted. I think about them every night. I just execute them every way possible that I can imagine. I used to be a peaceful sleeper. Now I sit up and throw punches in my sleep. I feel it should be me who kills them, no-one else has that right," Cobby said in the newspaper story.

His fondest memories of his wife, John Cobby told the *Mirror*, were during their holiday to Europe the year before her murder. He said their trip to Rome was Anita's favourite. The pair were strolling through the back streets when their umbrella broke. Saturated and lost, the two stumbled up to the Trevi Fountain. For three hours with the rain pelting down around them, Anita and John huddled together, surrounded by centuries of romance. "It was the most romantic time of my life and Anita loved Rome, especially that afternoon."

He said Anita's trusting innocence, her belief that nothing was ever wrong in the world, was the one thing about her he tried to change. He told of an incident that highlighted her unsuspecting nature. "We were kept awake all night in a tiny hotel room by a squeaky noise in the next room about every half hour. You could almost set your watch by it. It was driving Anita and I nuts. After a while I had a fair idea what it was but I had to check it out. Well, there in the hallway was this big Greek momma, obviously a prostitute working next door. I went back to Anita and she said to me in all sincerity, 'I've figured out what the noise is — it's a spinning wheel.' I just broke up. She thought someone was spinning wool when to anyone else the cause of the noise would have been obvious. She wouldn't have believed me if I'd tried to tell her anything else. She was really that naive."

All the media then wanted to know where John Cobby was. But, true to his word, he didn't break his silence again. The strain of doing it once had been too much.

Chapter 42

Shortly after the trial, Garry and Grace Lynch left Sydney behind to holiday with friends in Lavington, near Albury on the NSW-Victorian border. It was a chance for them to escape the media and spend some time together, time to take stock of their lives. The previous three months had been a terrible ordeal. They came back to Blacktown refreshed and Garry then set off alone to Lightning Ridge for some solitude while mining his opal claim.

On his return, Garry Lynch telephoned radio 2GB's breakfast host Mike Carlton to thank the public for their support. "It's sad that we can't answer all the beautiful letters and cards our family has had but many don't have addresses on them," he said. "We just want to say thank you very much for your support right through this deeply emotional time and God bless you all." He said one person had even offered to take the couple on a holiday to Norfolk Island. "This sort of kindness restores your faith in human nature. It reminds you there is still some goodness left in the world."

Then in July they took another trip. This time, Kathryn joined her parents on a trek through the Northern Territory. They planned to go back to Darwin, the city where they had been married. Then Kathryn would fly home to Sydney while Garry and Grace carried on to Western Australia to visit Grace's family. They drove hard, covering long distances each day to get to Ayers Rock, 240km from Alice Springs. "It was beautiful and we tackled the climb up the Rock," Garry recalled. "The girls were ahead of me but I felt good, like I was young again. Then I got to one of the landings and I felt this sharp pain in my chest. I thought, 'You old fool, you've overdone it.' But after a while I was alright and forgot about it."

The Lynchs were then off again, driving up through the Outback to Mataranka Springs, stopping to soak in the natural thermal pools before heading further on to Katherine. "We stopped in a caravan park by the river for the night," Garry said. "Early in the morning I staggered out of bed, bumping off things and crashing through the place as I went. I was slurring my words like I'd been drinking and my leg and arm just wouldn't move properly. Peg and Kathryn jumped up, but I convinced them that I was alright and they helped me back to bed. In the morning they made me go to Katherine Hospital." Garry Lynch had suffered a mild stroke. The strain of the past 18 months had finally taken a physical toll.

After three days in hospital Garry convinced doctors he was fit to leave. "It was like a miracle. Suddenly my leg and arm improved and my speech was only slightly affected. I wanted to go home. I remember feeling terrible about leaving my two girls stranded out in the middle of nowhere while I was in hospital." He and Kathryn shared the driving and took their time coming back to Sydney via the coast. The time had come in his life to rest.

One thing that amazed the Lynch family after the death of their daughter was the kindness of total strangers. They were deluged with mail. Some from people who knew Anita but many from people she had never met. "It was overwhelming," Garry recalled. "It kept us going. We had bagfuls of beautiful letters and cards and we had to answer them all. It kept us busy. We were finding out from people who knew Anita what a beautiful person she was. Of course we already knew how precious Anita was but to hear it from people whose lives she had touched was the most warming thing. And strangers who had been through similar tragedies to ours shared their experiences. It was the most gratifying feeling to know we weren't alone."

One message that especially touched their hearts was from an eight-year-old girl who left a note on Anita's grave at the Pine Grove Cemetery. Garry Lynch still becomes emotional when he speaks of the note, written in a childish hand, that they found on top of Anita's plaque. It read: "I suppose you are wondering who is the little girl visiting your grave every fortnight. My name is Cassandra and I am eight years old. My Poppy lies near you. I'm sure you know him now. When I visit Poppy I visit you and always bring you a flower the same as for Poppy. I've asked him to look after you. He'll make you smile with some of the funny things he says. Love Cassandra."

Garry and Grace Lynch never did meet Cassandra but they found her grandfather's grave not far from Anita's. On it was another note, to him, in the same childish hand.

Today, because of the changes in their lives since their daughter's death, the Lynchs believe the tragedy has strengthened their resolve and given them a new purpose. They say they have coped through their own strong religious beliefs and through the support of their friends and family. And because of their love for Anita. "At first it was true I felt such anger that I just wanted to tear somebody to pieces. Your emotions change all the time but you must turn them around to do some good. It's not an agony now because we have accepted the fact that our daughter isn't here anymore. Of course, little bubbles of it come up every now and again and it's sad, but she has a spiritual life now and we must get on with ours. You see, we've come to accept that this terrible thing *had* to happen, that we had to take a new direction in our lives, to help other people," Garry said. "It made us work for different things."

Now, Garry and Grace take an active interest in a number of support groups, set up to help the families of serious crime victims. Their strength, they hope, will give strength to other families. They are often called on to aid others in crisis. On one occasion Garry was asked to accompany the mother of a four-year-old murder victim to court when her husband was unable to attend. Little Tess DeBrincat had been gunned down from a passing car while she was inside her home.

Another time, the Lynchs went to comfort the heartbroken parents of 20-year-old bank clerk Janine Balding who was murdered in similar circumstances to Anita in September, 1988. Both Anita and Janine were abducted near railway stations by a group, and were stripped, raped and tortured, before they died within kilometres of each other. Janine was bound and gagged and drowned in a dam at Minchinbury, four kilometres from where Anita died. The man who headed the Balding investigation was Sgt Kevin Raue.

Now Garry Lynch is a member of the NSW Serious Offenders Review Board. He was invited to become the first civilian to sit on such a panel by NSW Premier Nick Greiner. It was hoped he would add a new dimension to the Board's decisions by representing the community. His colleagues are all professional men, judges and specialists in crime and punishment. In his new capacity Garry Lynch tours prisons throughout the state and speaks with many of the inmates. On his first day, the Board discussed the hunger strike of Michael Murphy, protesting against his transfer from Long Bay to Goulburn Gaol. He claimed the move put his life in danger. Garry Lynch excused himself from the discussion. The only proviso of the deal is that he must exempt himself should any of the five killers of his daughter appear before the Board.

"Life must go on," said Grace Lynch. "I don't think of Anita being up at the cemetery. I just have to look at her photograph or think of her and know she is near. She is with God now and they can't hurt her anymore."

Chapter 43

In 1987, Sgt Ian Kennedy was awarded the Police Commissioner's personal commendation "for outstanding leadership and dedication which resulted in the swift arrest" of the five men convicted of murdering Anita Cobby. NSW Police Commissioner John Avery also highly commended the actions of Sgt Graham Rosetta and Sgt Kevin Raue "for their excellent policemanship and the outstanding support" they gave during the inquiry. Commissioner Avery, after receiving advice from Kennedy, congratulated the entire team of detectives and uniformed police involved in the case for their superb work. He even passed on his thanks to the woman who typed the transcript for the Miss X tape recordings after Kennedy made special mention of her.

"The nature of this crime and the insensate actions of the offenders touched the hearts of all persons aware of this most despicable destruction of a fellow human being," the Commissioner said. "Therefore, as never before, the public looked towards this police force for swift and proper retribution against the perpetrators of this most atrocious offence. Without qualification, I am proud to say the members of this Police Department confronted with the task of arresting the offenders performed their duties with dedication and tenacity."

In 1989 Speed Kennedy was awarded the prestigious Australian Police Medal, for distinguished service. Presented by the Governor of NSW, the award was given partly because of Kennedy's work during the Cobby case.

One of the most touching stories of the investigation was also one of its best kept secrets. Two of the officers working on the case began relationships with Anita's nursing friends Lyn Bradshaw and Elaine Bray. Colleagues of the couples said nothing as the relationships developed, mainly out of respect for the four and also because they had all been through so much turmoil that the extra attention the media would surely give them wasn't wanted. Constable Paul Davies and Lyn Bradshaw now have a baby daughter, Ashleigh. Lyn remarked recently, "If anything good has come out of this terrible, tragic thing, then it is this baby. If we hadn't gone through all this then we wouldn't have our beautiful daughter."

After John Travers was charged with murdering Anita Cobby, the lives of his family became hellish. They received death threats, his brothers and sisters were harassed and the ailing Sharon Travers was forced to live a reclusive lifestyle, rarely venturing outside the house. Her neighbours would do her grocery shopping for her while her children paid her bills. Even visits to doctors became a chore and she preferred to skip them than feel the embarrassment of being pointed out as the mother of John Travers. "Cars pull up outside the house at all hours of the night just to have a look where John lived," Sharon Travers said. "People have come into the backyard and once we were all woken up by a terribly loud banging on the door at midnight. And when I reported my car stolen, just after John was picked up, they just laughed."

But it was the persecution of her family that devastated Sharon Travers. It made her cry almost every time. One son found it difficult to hold down jobs after it became known who his brother was, and once Brock was "pushed out of his wheelchair at school because the other kids said his brother was a murderer". Sharon recalled the time her daughter Lisa and two-year-old granddaughter Tracey-Lee were at a bus stop. "This woman came up and said, 'You're that murderer's sister!' I'd always told Lisa to ignore them and walk away. Well, the woman picked on Tracey-Lee and gave her a shove, making her fall over and hit her head on the gutter. Lisa lost her cool and thumped the woman, wouldn't you?"

The lack of action taken over her son's behaviour by government departments when he was growing up left Sharon Travers bitter. "When he was in trouble for jigging school or smoking marijuana, all that he would ever get was a rap across the knuckles," she lamented. "And the institutions they sent him to were more like holiday camps. I don't think parents can be held responsible for what their children can do because they grow up and grow away from you."

With a staunch love that only a mother could have, Sharon Travers would not accept that her son killed Anita Cobby. "I believe he *believes* he did it, but I don't." She cried whenever the subject was raised. "I asked him once, 'John, just tell me (if you did it)' and he said, 'Leave it alone.' He told me not to read the paper or watch the TV. 'It's a load of shit,' he said. You see, if he had been drinking and smoking as they say he had been, then I'm sorry, he couldn't have done it. I know my son. He would pass out for hours, you couldn't wake him for six or seven hours whenever he got on the drink or drugs. I think from the little bits he heard from the others later on he thinks he must have done it. I will never believe it for a minute."

When pressed about her reason for believing her son didn't kill Anita, she would only say, "They took a vow and they set him up. I have my own suspicions but I'm not going to say."

Sharon Travers confided to family members that she believed there were another two men present on the night of the murder. The investigating police emphatically deny the allegations, saying the evidence overwhelmingly showed the five were the only ones involved. "None of the men mentioned a sixth or seventh person but all gave identical lists of who was there," Ian Kennedy said. Miss X, too, was quick to deny these rumours. "John only told me four other names and if he was going to protect anyone else it would have been Mick Murdoch," she said. "After all, he was John's best friend."

Once in prison, Travers cut himself off from his family, often refusing visits. As one prison officer commented, "He just wanted to be left alone, to settle down to the business of serving his time." Sharon Travers said he had asked her not to visit because, "It's too painful for him. He'd always known how I felt about what he was up to (his life of crime). I'd say, 'Where have you been?' and he'd just say, 'What you don't know won't hurt you'."

Sharon Travers said not a day went by when she didn't think about the family of Anita Cobby. She had often considered going to see them or writing, to let them know she was so sorry for what had happened to their daughter. "But my friends said no, to leave them alone, it wasn't going to make any difference anyway. At least they have a chance to let go of their child, they buried their daughter. I'm mourning a kid that isn't even dead. He'll never be free, he'll never have a family or enjoy Christmas, weddings and other things families do. You might as well says he's dead, only there's no gravestone."

Sharon Travers died the week before Christmas, 1989, from complications arising from Cushings Syndrome. She was 39. A friend believed she died of a broken heart. "She felt so much guilt for the suffering her other children went through. She died from a broken heart over John."

John Travers was allowed to attend his mother's funeral on Friday, December 22, at the Pine Grove Cemetery, where his victim, Anita Cobby, is buried. He was dressed in a dark suit, tie and heavy sunglasses. He told other prisoners it was his "Godfather's outfit". He wore a metal restraining belt around his waist with handcuffs threaded through it at the front and was accompanied by four prison officers. So strict was the security, Travers was unable to speak with his family or other mourners during the 30-minute ceremony but he was allowed several minutes beside his mother's coffin before it was removed for burial.

The decision to allow Travers to attend the funeral was not taken lightly and NSW Corrective Services Minister Michael Yabsley conferred with Travers' gaol superintendent and psychologists before he gave the go-ahead. A spokesman from his office said later, "As with all such cases we just had to look at where the prisoner is, where the funeral is being held and the logistics of planning a high level security operation. But the Department does realise that compassion is needed in the prison system and in this case it was decided it was in the interests of the prisoner to be allowed to attend."

The same considerations had been given when Michael Murdoch attended the funeral of his mother Rose in September, 1989. Rose Murdoch died after contracting emphysema. She believed in the innocence of her son to the end. He, too, was separated from his family during the service and was unable to speak with other mourners. Michael Murdoch wore the navy blue suit his mother had bought him so he'd look his best in court.

The Murphys are not a close family. In fact the Cobby case, and the life sentences passed against three of the brothers, have driven a wedge between them all. Les and Dulcie Murphy live apart.

One of the girls, Marie, has isolated herself from them, rarely seeing the family. Les Murphy senior has a poor relationship with the son named after him but visits Gary and Michael occasionally when they are in Sydney prisons. Dulcie Murphy will only visit Les and has told family members she blames Mick for the others being in prison. Dulcie's elderly mother is heartbroken about her favourite grandson Michael's imprisonment but is too old to travel and it would be too distressing for her to visit him in gaol. Brother Bernie won't even speak about Mick while Pat, serving time on an armed robbery charge, has changed his name, even though most inmates know he is the brother of Michael, Gary and Les Murphy. The offspring of the Murphy brothers have little to do with their fathers. Michael Murphy has a 14-year-old daughter, Kelley, and he has told her mother it is in the best interests of the child not to see him in prison. He is still upset that during the hunt for him, police raiding their house allegedly held a gun to his daughter's head while they searched. (Police vehemently deny this.) The daughter once told a television host, "My daddy is not a murderer, he's innocent." Now Kelley lives with her maternal grandparents after her mother was gaoled. Michael Murphy still maintains his innocence. "There's lots of things that didn't come up in the trial," he said recently. "I'm hoping I can still prove I didn't do it. I was railroaded." Gary Murphy's two children have no contact with their father. Their mother has changed their names. Les Murphy's small daughter Tracey-Lee is often brought to the prison to visit her father.

Chapter 44

Every second week, Kerrie Sandberg has a friend look after her two young sons, Scott and Brendan, for a few hours. She mounts her pushbike, carrying a plastic bag, and peddles the six kilometres to Pine Grove Cemetery. She wheels her bike up the winding path and across the picturesque lawns until she reaches an oblong plaque, neatly set in the ground. Sitting on the grass she unpacks a toothbrush, a bottle of Brasso and a soft cloth and then sets to work.

She often thinks about the first time she met Anita Cobby, then a single girl selling raffle tickets with her parents to raise money for the Miss Australia Quest at Westfield Mall at Parramatta. Kerrie worked in the shopping centre then and was about to have her first baby. She was a single mum. Kerrie remembers her surprise when Anita and her parents arrived at the hospital with flowers and some baby clothes for her. She had only just met them. Anita had adored the baby.

How could she forget the reeling sensation that hit her the moment she saw the newspaper photo of Anita Cobby, and the headline that said she was the woman who had been so brutally and randomly murdered at Prospect. It was *her* Anita. She had felt so lost, so hurt. Anita was always happy and making other people feel good.

After 20 minutes at the graveside her job is done. The plaque on Anita Cobby's grave will always gleam. This is a fortnightly ritual Kerrie Sandberg feels she must keep for the rest of her life. It is a labour of appreciation for having been lucky enough to have had her life touched, if only briefly, by Anita Lorraine Cobby.

POSTSCRIPT

On April 28, 1986, a memorial service was held in the historic Sydney Hospital chapel to unveil a plaque dedicated to the memory of Anita Cobby. Nearly 150 people joined Garry, Grace and Kathryn for the 15-minute ceremony, including Const Debbie Wallace and five Blacktown detectives. Rev Jonathon Holland told the assembly that the dedication of the plaque "is a tangible expression of the depth of love felt for her. It is hoped all good of Anita's example will be preserved here (at the hospital)." He also announced that the hospital had established a nurse's education scholarship to be known as the Anita Cobby Memorial Fund.

Garry and Grace held hands as 17-year-old Dorrigo teenager Paul Burbridge who, as a patient, could testify to Anita's loving care, unveiled the plaque on the sandstone wall. Anita had nursed him for many months at Coffs Harbour and later at Sydney Hospital after he was injured in a car accident.

At the bottom of the plaque are five words. They read: "May her light shine forever."

ACKNOWLEDGEMENTS

The events in this book have been recorded with the kind assistance of family, friends, neighbours and associates of the people involved. Scenes have been recreated only when information is corroborated or given by a reliable source. As well, court and police records, newspaper stories, photographs, television and radio reports have been used.

I gratefully acknowledge the assistance of the many people who cannot or do not wish to be named, including members of the legal profession, nurses, journalists, photographers, the NSW Corrective Services Department, the NSW Family and Community Services Department and the NSW Police Department.

In particular I thank Grace, Kathryn and Garry Lynch and their family who have given generously of their time and thoughts throughout the writing of this book and made available photos from their family album.

Thanks, too, to Anne Farmer, Miss X, Sgt Ian Kennedy, Graham Rosetta, Sgt Chris O'Toole, Det Const Paul Davies, Det Sen Const Garry Heskett, Sgt Stan Szostak, Sen Const Paul Hamilton, Sgt Phil Gaspert, Felicity Moffatt, Sandra Harvey, Norm Lipson, Sean Flannery, Simon Bouda, John Choueifate, Steve Barrett, Adam Walters, Tim Stone, Jenny Hughes, Karen Hood, Lyn Bradshaw, Channel TEN and Channel 7, Bill Edmonds and my workmates at Channel TEN for their invaluable help and support. Also, I am grateful to the members of the Four-Em-Tee for their friendship over the years.

Most importantly, I thank my wonderful husband Phillip Sigsworth for his care and support during the project, and my family – the Sheppards and the Sigsworths – specifically my mother Joan and my father John. Also Syd Griffith, for his never-ending advice and availability, Kevin for his support and time.